ROOM *for* DOUBT

ROOM

for

DOUBT

Wendy Lesser

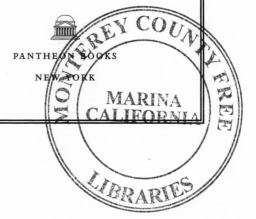

PANTHEON BOOKS

NEW YORK

Library of Congress Cataloging-in-Publication Data

Lesser, Wendy.
Room for doubt / Wendy Lesser.

p.   cm.

ISBN 978-0-375-42400-7

1. Lesser, Wendy.   2. Periodical editors—United States—
Biography.   3. Critics—United States—Biography.   I. Title.
PN4874.L3785A3 2007   810.9—dc22   [B]   2006043672

www.pantheonbooks.com

Printed in the United States of America
First Edition

2   4   6   8   9   7   5   3   1

For Katharine

Contents

Acknowledgments

During the period when I was working on this book, I received fellowships from the American Academy in Berlin, Princeton University, the Remarque Institute at New York University, and the Cullman Center for Scholars and Writers at the New York Public Library. I also got helpful advice and commentary from a number of readers, including Barbara and Martin Bauer, Deirdre and Allen Bergson, Sara Bershtel, Tim Clark, Dan Frank, Geoffrey Hartman, Arthur Lubow, Katharine Ogden Michaels, Adam Phillips, and Christopher Ricks. I am very grateful for both kinds of support.

For the David Hume section, I consulted a variety of secondary sources, biographical as well as philosophical. Among the most important of these were J. Y. T. Grieg's two-volume edition of *The Letters of David Hume* and his biography *David Hume;* Ernest Campbell Mossner's *The Life of David Hume* and *The Forgotten Hume;* T. H. Green's and T. H. Grose's annotated edition of Hume's *Essays Moral, Political, and Literary*; Alasdair MacIntyre's introduction to his selected *Hume's Ethical Writings*; A. J. Ayer's *Hume*; Norman Kemp Smith's *The Philosophy of David Hume*; and *The Cambridge Companion to Hume*, edited by David Fate Norton.

My errors, of course, are completely my own.

Part One

OUT OF
BERLIN

I expected to go a lifetime without ever setting foot in Germany. When I first began traveling to Europe as a college student, it was Ireland, Britain, Holland, France, and Italy that I ended up visiting—neither wholly by chance nor wholly by choice, but in that drifty, in-between way college students do things. Afterwards, when I was living in England for two years, it would have been easy enough to go to Germany, but I didn't. And then, as I grew into my thirties and forties, this coincidence hardened into a resolve. "I have never been to Germany" became one of the totemic sentences of my identity, like "I have never been to a professional ball game" or "I have never been sky-diving." *And never will,* these sentences implied.

But of course Germany was a different case. Nothing prevented me from attending ball games or taking up sky-diving except fear—fear of crowds and boredom in the former instance, just plain fear in the latter. The feeling that kept me away from Germany, while it had elements of fear mingled into it, was much more complicated. It partook of moral distaste and historical allegiance. It stemmed from a notion that Jews do not visit Germany, and broadened out to include all morally upright people in its scope. I found myself unduly shocked when friends of mine reported that they had enjoyed their trips to Germany. "Shocked" is perhaps not the right word: I found it incomprehensible that one could have a good time there. And since pleasure (though sometimes a very abstruse pleasure, of a sort that other people might call work) is what fuels all my travel decisions, I couldn't imagine ever wanting to go to Germany.

My Jewishness, though it clearly had something to do with this attitude, was not enough to explain it. I am not and have never been a very good Jew. Born into a family of secular Jews in which religious disbelief went back several generations, I grew up celebrating Christmas and attending school on Jewish holidays, as did most of the other California Jews I knew; in fact, we were all so assimilated that I barely knew which of my childhood friends were Jewish and which were not. On my father's side, there had once been some synagogue-going by my grandfather, but that, I suspect, was largely for business purposes: as a child, I was told that this grandfather had been sent to San Quentin for selling land that didn't exist "to other members of the synagogue," a description which managed to suggest that the crime inhered mainly in the tribal betrayal. My father's reaction to having a father like this was to become scrupulously rule-abiding and unshakably agnostic.

My mother's relationship to Judaism was slightly more mystical. Her parents—a Russian-Jewish woman, staunchly tough and unremittingly difficult during all the years I knew her, who had wanted to be a doctor but had been channeled by anti-Semitism and anti-feminism into nursing; and a man about whom I have no information except that his name was Ephraim Gerson, that he abandoned his family when the children were young, and that he joined the Communist Party shortly before dying of alcoholism—had no religious feelings whatsoever. Perhaps because of this, my mother longed to see what religious belief felt like. She would introduce into our family bizarre versions of Jewish practice in an attempt to simulate the real thing. At one point she insisted we have a Passover seder, and when the Haggadah specified that a ceremonial bone be placed on the table, she went out to the backyard and fetched in the family dog's chewed-up bone. One year she attempted to ban Christmas from the house. (I cannot remember whether my sister and I overcame the ban that year, or only the following year.) Her second marriage, to a non-Jew, was conducted by a rabbi. None of these attempts were viewed by either me or my sister as serious efforts to inculcate us with religion. And the result, in my case, is that I am a devout atheist who acknowledges her Jewish ancestry mainly because it would seem to be caving in to Hitler not to do so.

Hitler was a definite presence in my childhood. Though he was already seven years dead by the time I was born, he lived on in the collective imagination as the ultimate incarnation of evil. Among people my age, he was the endpoint of every philosophical argument ("Well, would you believe in the death penalty if it were *Hitler* being executed?") and a useful spur to action (when I ran fast in schoolyard races, I always imagined being chased by the Nazis). In our secular household he stood in for the devil, but he was much more effective than the devil, in that his works were undeniable. Among the pictures in our family photograph albums was a yellowing news photo my mother had preserved from her youth, a picture of a Jewish child looking straight at the camera as she was herded off to a concentration camp. Though she looked as if she could have been related to us, she was not: all our relatives (with whom, in any case, we were mostly not on speaking terms) were safely in America by the time of Hitler's rise to power. But it was made clear to me that he *would* have come after me if he could have. Being merely Jew-*ish,* as Jonathan Miller puts it, would not have been enough to save me.

We were not the kind of family that boycotted all things German. Our cars were Volkswagen Bugs, we had a recording of Lotte Lenya singing *The Threepenny Opera,* and one of the few things my mother taught me to cook was a raisin-studded noodle *kugel,* identical in its title and contents to the dish made by a Lutheran friend I met at college. But the strange thing is that when German things did seep into our household, I always faintly imagined they were Jewish. It was not until I was well into adulthood, for instance, that I realized Bertolt Brecht was not a Jew.

These misperceptions of mine were not entirely wrong. One of the things I was to discover, when I eventually went to Berlin, was how deeply Jewish that city's culture still is. Or perhaps what I observed is how deeply the German and Jewish cultures had once entered into each other, so that the versions we now have of them, at least here in America and there in Berlin, are still colored by that mutual infusion. It's not just a matter of language, though it's true that for an urban, coastal American, German words are mostly familiar because they sound like Yiddish. And it's not just that many Jews used to live in Berlin (seventy percent of the city's lawyers, I've read, and ninety percent of its doctors, or perhaps it was the other way around, were Jewish in 1930). The real oddity lies in the number of things about the city that still feel Jewish: for instance, its passion for concert-hall performances—for art and culture in any of their manifestations, really; or its insistence on punctuality; or the blunt, practical manner of its inhabitants. Arriving in Berlin, I felt in some strange way as if I were coming to a homeland I'd never known about, a place where people shared all my personal quirks. My love of order, my brusque aggressiveness, my linear mode of thought, my insistence on constantly distinguishing better from worse, all blended in with the surrounding culture rather than marking me off as a weirdo, as they had in California. Some of these qualities could have, and did, find fellowship in New York, but that did not surprise me: Jews still lived there, after all. What amazed me was that even more of these Jewish traits of mine (if they were indeed Jewish, and not just mysteriously, inexplicably German) found a roost, a homecoming, in this city from which the Jews had mainly disappeared.

There were lots of Jews, though, where I was staying in Berlin—at the American Academy, out in Wannsee.

When I say "lots," I mean proportionally: of the twelve or fourteen fellows who were there when I was, five of us were Jews and a sixth, though nominally Christian, did most of his research in Jewish Studies. The large house in which the Academy was located had once been owned by a wealthy Berlin Jew named Hans Arnhold, and the fellowship program was still partially subsidized by the Arnhold heirs in New York, all of whom had left Germany with plenty of time to spare. The director of the American Academy was a Texas Jew, Gary Smith, who had married into a prominent Jewish-connected German family (his wife, the daughter of a former mayor of Berlin, had actually converted to Judaism in her youth) and who tended to run the Academy as if it were a version of his own extended clan. At Yom Kippur, for instance, he asked around the dining room to see who would want tickets to services. ("Are you Jewish?" he asked me, in his hurried search for possible ticket-needers. "How can you even *ask?*" responded one of my fellow fellows, a Leningrad-born Jew who could perceive the lineaments of my Russian grandmother's face in mine.) As Christmas approached, all the other houses on our street sported a profusion of lights and decorations, in the traditional Berlin manner; only our grand property remained austerely bare.

The townlet of Wannsee, which managed to be both

part of and apart from the city of Berlin, had its own complicated history. The last outpost of West Berlin during the days of the Wall, it sat on a beautiful string of lakes which at that time divided western Berlin from East Germany. Earlier, in the 1920s, Wannsee had been a pastoral suburb where many Jews and other Berliners had large weekend houses. (One such Jewish family, the department-store-owning Landauers, are featured in Christopher Isherwood's slightly fictionalized *Goodbye to Berlin*.) In between these two periods, it was the site of the notorious Wannsee Conference, at which Hitler's henchmen arrived at the Final Solution. The Wannsee Conference House, now a museum detailing the Nazi extermination of the Jews, had a strange dual role in my Berlin life. On the one hand, it was just a physical place, not quite visible from my balcony but easily accessible via a short bus ride, a specific location from which you could start a lovely lakeside walk to Potsdam or Peacock Island. ("Meet me outside the Final Solution House," you might say to a friend with whom you were planning an afternoon excursion.) And on the other hand it was a specter, a monstrous thing, a building that I actually refused to set foot inside during my entire time there, because even though I no longer believe in the concept of evil (it has been debased by its recent appearances in

American political language, and besides, I deplore its religious overtones), I felt something very much like evil emanating from that house, the one time I stood close to it and peered through the gates.

Many visitors to Berlin, and not just Jews, had what I considered an unhealthy desire to wallow in the recent history of extermination. People were always telling me about one or another not-to-be-missed monument: the preserved train tracks out by the Grünwald S-Bahn station, where each plaque recorded the number of Jews deported that day; or the in-progress Holocaust memorial, a set of tombstone-like cubes dotting a patch of barren ground between Potsdamer Platz and the Brandenburg Gate; or the recently completed Jewish Museum, designed by that self-promoting master of the Architecture of Victims school, Daniel Libeskind. I did, against my own better judgment, visit the Jewish Museum (an artily off-kilter structure whose sense of "dislocation" is more suited to a modern-art museum than a monument to the displaced), and I was deeply offended, as I suspected I would be, by its grotesque breast-beating. "This way to the Memory Void!" trumpeted the Disneyesque signs leading me into the Holy of Holies of remembrance— and then, when I got there, I was expected to walk on the flat metallic "faces" of symbolic dead Jews. This I declined to do, and, fleeing through room after room of exhibits about European Jews and their sufferings and achievements, I focused on converting my sense of unease into an ethical theory. A system of morality, I decided, was only truly moral if it was based on a certain degree of impersonality, of detachment. It was impossible to act in the world as if we identified with everyone equally, but ethical behavior demanded that we at least make the effort to act in this way. I felt, therefore, morally offended by all this championing of the Jews, all this elaboration of the wrongs done to *them alone,* as if those were the only wrongs that mattered. Or so I told myself at the time. It's also the case that I, personally, didn't need to be told what the Germans did to the Jews. It was the one thing I knew about them before I got to Berlin; it is the only thing that many Americans my age know about the Germans. I was there to find something else.

I would not, probably, have been so willing to look for that something else had I not been persuaded of the Germans' sense of self-recrimination. In their own eyes, and not just the eyes of the world, the Germans are the people who murdered six million Jews. The poet C. K. Williams, who stayed at the American Academy in Berlin five years before I did, has written a very smart essay about the fact that the Germans and the Jews are alike now because they are both "symbolic" people. I won't try to recapitulate his argument, since he has put his case more elegantly and lucidly than I could, but I will use its sharp central idea, which I think is both true and not true, to hone my own amorphous thoughts. Yes, the Jews and the Germans are now joined at the hip, historically and morally. And yes, what they have in common is something to do with abstraction as a way of viewing entire populations: both Jews and Germans are now seen, even by themselves, as if from the outside. But there is a huge difference between viewing yourself as special because you have generally and particularly been persecuted, and viewing yourself as special because you were once a terrible persecutor. The former does not demand an ethical response; the latter does. Jews do not, and should not, need to examine their own beliefs or activities to discover why the Third Reich did what it did to them, but Germans *do* need, and *have* needed, to conduct this kind of rigorous self-examination. And the result is a society that is acutely and unremittingly self-conscious about ethical behavior.

This is an entirely different thing from being the homeland of Kant, Hegel, and Nietzsche; it is ethical philosophy of a very practical kind. There is a level of moral awareness that invades everything in the country's daily existence, from the way it is governed to how people act toward each other on trains. I am not saying that this scrupulosity has resulted in the perfection of human nature. On the contrary, it has not even succeeded in wiping out anti-Semitism (not to mention other forms of racial prejudice) in Germany. But what it *has* done is to produce a nation of people who are very much alive to their own capacity for unforgivable behavior—a capacity, they have learned, that is completely in keeping with being a nice, civilized, conventional sort of person in ordinary life. It is this knowledge about their own darkest side which made the Germans seem so admirable to me.

I felt this very strongly on the day I was taken, with a handful of other Academy fellows and staff, on a visit to the Reichstag's art collection. I had seen the Reichstag before, in its more public aspects: the imposing façade with its inscription "To the German People"; the lovely, airy, vertiginous dome from which you can get the best views of surrounding Berlin; and the vast chamber, with its cantilevered balconies and purplish-blue upholstery, where the parliamentary delegates meet. But the art collection is housed in more intimate parts of the building, those in which the parliament does its routine business. One aspect, in fact, of that routine business is the selection and commissioning of the Reichstag's art, a job which is done entirely by a subcommittee of elected delegates—the art committee being one of the regular parliamentary assignments, just as Appropriations or Armed Services might be in America. These delegates may listen to the advice of art critics or art historians while they are coming to their decision, but they argue the issues and cast their votes on their own, with no expert intervention.

What they had voted for, thus far, included a number of monumental works that kept before the delegates' eyes, on a daily basis, the darkest moments of recent German history. One particularly memorable piece by Christian Boltanski, for instance, consisted of facing walls of rectangular plaques (reminiscent, in their slightly corroded appearance, of the stacked drawers of cremated ashes one might find in an old cemetery) naming all the previous members of the German parliament: those who had been killed by the Nazis were marked in a special way, and the era from 1933 to 1945 was represented simply by a black space. Every delegate to the present parliament had to pass by these walls daily on the way into the voting chamber.

Another installation, this one in an inner courtyard visible from all the flanking windows, featured a rather endearingly and very un-Teutonically messy garden, in which was embedded a series of luminous letters. The garden (which the curators were forbidden to modify in any way, unless its growth began to obscure the letters) had sprung up from seeds brought by the delegates from their various districts; and the letters (which caused such a controversy that the entire parliament, and not just the art committee, had to vote on this commission) spelled out the German words for "To the Population." This phrase, which clearly alluded to all the non-citizens and non-Aryans who had come to reside in present-day Germany, was intended by the artist, Hans Haacke, as a direct response to the outer façade's more exclusive "Dem Deutschen Volke."

These are not, either of them, exactly my favorite kind of artwork, but in their place, and arising as they had arisen, they seemed to me just right. I was moved by the earnestness and honesty with which they had been selected, and by the quiet power the finished works emanated. And I couldn't help thinking, as I looked at them, how differently we do things in America, where oblivion and cultivated ignorance are the government's chief mechanisms for getting through the day, and where commemoration of our national misdeeds—especially through any kind of publicly funded art—would seem to be unthinkable.

My other exemplary experience of German moral scrupulousness took place on the Berlin trains. I spent a lot of time on the trains in Berlin, partly because Wannsee was so far from the center, but also because the public transportation system was itself a work of art, with S-Bahn, U-Bahn, bus, and railroad lines all blending together to create a practical, punctual, far-reaching network that could take you anywhere you wanted to go. You could buy a one-month pass starting on any day you chose, and it allowed you, for something in the range of sixty or seventy dollars (less if you were unemployed), to ride any bus, train, or subway in the city. The beauty part was that you didn't have to show your *Monatskarte* to a ticket-taker or pass it through a machine: you just kept it with you and flashed it when asked, which might happen twice in a day or only once in three weeks, depending on how many conductors were riding your trains. This in turn meant that you could leap aboard any train or bus just as it pulled in, without taking the time to fumble for a ticket (or waiting for other people to fumble for theirs). In that vast majority of moments when you were not being asked to show your pass, it was as if you owned the city's transportation system and could ride anywhere for free. A certain code of honor needed to prevail, of course, but that it *did* prevail was evident in the fact that even teenage punks—pierced, tattooed, and swigging whiskey directly from the bottle—scrambled to retrieve their *Monatskarten* when the conductor came through. I found the whole system liberating and delightful, and said so repeatedly, to the point where visiting friends accused me of being a paid employee of Berlin Public Transport.

The particular incident I found so instructive happened late one night on the regional express, as my husband and I were going back out to Wannsee. We had previously remarked to each other on the rude behavior of Berliners in crowded compartments—the way they would, for instance, put their backpacks or packages on the seat next to them, and not remove them even if you eyed the seat balefully or longingly; you had to ask if the seat was free in order to get it. (This wasn't just discrimination against foreigners, either: most of the time I saw it happen, the seatless petitioner was another German.) But that night we saw a different kind of train behavior. The express, which normally ran all the way to Potsdam, had come to an unexpected halt in Charlottenburg. The public address system announced that we should all get off the train and cross the platform so as to catch the next train out. My German wasn't good enough for me to figure out exactly what was happening, but at least my husband and I knew enough to get off the train. One young guy, though, his ears completely covered by head-phones, was left behind on the empty express. He leaned sleepily against the window, oblivious to his fate, and we were just beginning to wonder what would happen to him when one of those heavyset German women, the kind who habitually took up one and sometimes *two* extra seats with her packages, went back to the train and rapped loudly on the outside of his window. He looked up, startled, and took in the woman's gestured instruc-tions just in time to get himself across the platform to the waiting train.

Later, we reported this incident to a German friend of ours, a man who was born in West Germany in 1956 and who made his living editing a leftwing magazine. We contrasted the boorishness of the casual seat-hogging behavior with the public attentiveness of the late-night warning to the stranger on a train. "No way," we said, "would you call that kind of attention to yourself at mid-night on the New York subways. If some strange guy was about to miss his train, you'd just let him."

Martin's explanation of the incident drew on his own

postwar schooldays. "We were always taught," he said, "that if someone is in trouble, indifference is not a sufficient response. You cannot just look the other way. Because we had seen what could happen when people *did* look the other way."

I have since told this story to a number of German-Americans, both Jews and non-Jews, and they tend to interpret the incident differently. Rather than enthusing about the woman's public-spiritedness, they see her behavior as a sign of typical German officiousness, or rule-mongering, or excessive orderliness, or some other unpleasant national characteristic. And no doubt those qualities do enter into it. But Martin's view rings truer to the feeling I had at the time: that she was actively, disinterestedly, and somewhat selflessly saving the boy from the fate that would otherwise have befallen him. The impersonality of her gesture—the fact that, as an individual, he meant nothing in particular to her—was precisely part of its charm.

I do not actually have a feel for Germany as a whole, since I barely spent any time outside of Berlin. Berliners themselves think of their city as a special case, and I agree with them. I suspect that even if I never live there again, I will feel uncannily and permanently attached to it.

It is not an inherently lovable city. It is not beautiful like Paris or San Francisco, not exciting like London or New York, not charming like Barcelona. Its greatest charm may even be this very lack of charm, this blunt refusal to manipulate and cajole—just as certain people can be charming because they are so evidently *not* trying to charm. And, as with such people, you feel about Berlin that it is your discovery alone, that you are the only one who really sees it well enough to love it, since it is not asking to be loved.

In many neighborhoods of Berlin, you can walk for blocks—nay, miles—without coming upon a picturesque sight. It's true that there are some wonderful examples of modern architecture, Mies van der Rohe's Neue Nationalgalerie and Norman Foster's Reichstag Dome being perhaps the best; and there are also a few lovely older buildings, like Schinkel's grand Konzerthaus in the Gendarmenmarkt. It's also true that the city has a vast amount of green space, which makes it surprisingly livable on a daily basis (a factor which was even more important in the days when West Berliners, hemmed in by the Wall, couldn't simply drive out to the nearby countryside). But there is no quaint medieval quarter, no hill with views, and very little, aside from the areas around Fasanenplatz and Kollwitzplatz, that is built on a comfortably human yet densely urban scale.

Much of Berlin was bombed out of existence during the Second World War, and even more succumbed to redevelopment in the years since then, so that almost nothing is left, in a physical sense, of Christopher Isherwood's or George Grosz's Berlin, not to mention Theodor Fontane's or Adolph Menzel's nineteenth-century city.

And yet something of the spirit of that old city survives—not as a preserved bit of architecture or landscape, but as a feeling, a possibility. Berlin is a place that is always in the process of becoming something else. Its primary allegiance is to change, to novelty, to self-invention or reinvention. But this constant transformation is mysteriously and eternally anchored to the solid rock of history. Berlin never forgets its own past, and it never lets *you* forget it. So all the newness you see there is self-consciously displayed against the invisible oldness whose place it has taken. Whether it's the Berlin Wall or a Jewish synagogue, the Royal Palace or a tree-lined street, the absent structure refuses to give way entirely to the present one that has usurped its position. Or perhaps it would be more accurate to say that even the present-day buildings—some of them huge and overbearing in the extreme—carry with them the whiff of their own mortality, the sense (unusual in modern-day skyscrapers) that they will someday disappear, just like the constructions that preceded them.

If Venice, say, is about timelessness, then Berlin is about a very particular moment in time: *this* moment, the moment you happen to be there, which is singularly apparent to you because it is so evidently distinct from the historical moments on either side of it. Living in Berlin, you picture its past and also its future, so that you have no hope (as you might imagine you have in most other cities) of holding onto the place you have fallen in love with. Before you have time to act on that love—learn German, buy an apartment, find local employment—the city will have changed, becoming something other than what you thought you had finally found. Just as the construction cranes define the skyline, throwing up new buildings between one week and the next, the rapidity of all the other kinds of change forces you to acknowledge that the word "finally" has no place in Berlin.

Arriving there in 2003, I was very much aware of the precise historical moment I inhabited. In Germany, the Wall had been down for fourteen years, Berlin had once again become the capital, the euro had recently replaced the Deutsche Mark, and Gerhard Schroeder's leftish central government was struggling with the effects of hav-

ing swallowed East Germany whole. The place I came
from was at a particular juncture, too: it was an America
which, six months into its invasion of Iraq, was run by
the most venally rightwing administration of my adult
life. The voters in my home state of California were
about to elect a movie-star muscle-man as governor, the
best newspaper in the country was effectively reducing
its culture pages to pap, and television consisted increasingly of lurid reality shows that bore no relation to
anyone's idea of reality. The shock of going from one
culture to the other was intense, and bracing, but it was
also rather terrifying to be able to see myself and everything else so clearly from the outside, as if I were a character in history.

By the time I got to Berlin, the only visible piece of the
Wall was a preserved chunk of it not far from Potsdamer
Platz, a thin, puny, pathetic-looking remnant that didn't
seem as if it would have kept anybody from going anywhere. The vast acres of no-man's-land that had previously stretched between East and West Berlin had been
completely filled in by construction, most of it high-end
shopping and office buildings. Friedrichstrasse Station,
once the heavily guarded exit from East Berlin, was now

the busy center of my beloved transportation network. Physically, the city felt unified. And yet virtually all Berliners over the age of twenty-five or so routinely referred to neighborhoods as being in the "former East" or the "former West," and in fact continued to view themselves as coming originally from West or East Germany. The traces of this recent past (and all it entailed, ideologically, socially, economically) were very much a part of the living present, even for newcomers like me whose experience of it was entirely secondhand. It gave the citizens a rich collective memory of self-division, and this in turn meant that the performing arts, which in Berlin still very much relied on concepts like "dialectic" and "alienation," had something quite specific on which to draw.

I saw many performances that hinged on this recent history, but two in particular stood out. One was a production of Beethoven's *Fidelio* at the Komische Oper. Of the three professional opera companies in Berlin, the Komische has always defined itself as the most local: it catered to its relatively unworldly East German audience by translating every opera into German, and was still, in 2003, adhering to this linguistic rule (though that did not, of course, affect *Fidelio*). The building itself bore its history in layers, with a Victorian jewel-box of an auditorium set inside a garishly modern lobby-snackbar-cloakroom structure that dated from the postwar Communist era. And the night I was there, even the audience members looked, to my eye, different from those at the placidly bourgeois Deutsche Oper or the comparatively hip Staatsoper: they seemed more dressed-up than the latter, less comfortable in their dressed-up clothes than the former.

I went with a friend from the Academy who spoke German fluently and who had already been to the Komische a number of times, both before and after 1989. The production itself (performed to a half-empty theater on a Saturday night, with a brave soprano fighting off a cold) was described in its own one-page program as being Brechtian, and it was indeed truer to that method—of performers morphing into characters and back again, of history visibly presented, of art that simultaneously moved you and made you think—than anything I saw at the Berliner Ensemble. The singing was very good and the acting was unusually persuasive, but what made me feel I was really seeing something for the first time was the utter conviction with which the actor-singers conveyed their Romantic-era story of imprisonment and liberation.

"Can you tell what they're doing?" my friend asked

me as the first-act curtain came down. I thought about the cheap street-clothes the performers wore, and the massive, slightly abstract set which created an impassable barrier out of functioning stage machinery, and the answer came to me without a pause. "East Berlin," I said, and my friend nodded.

The other occasion on which the past seemed particularly alive was a concert given by the Maryinsky Orchestra and Chorus, under the charismatic and somewhat unnerving leadership of Valery Gergiev. Visiting from St. Petersburg as part of a major German–Russian cultural exchange, the orchestra performed two pieces of Russian music, both of them written in 1936: Prokofiev's Cantata for the Twentieth Anniversary of the October Revolution, and Shostakovich's Symphony Number 4. In choosing the Prokofiev, Gergiev must have known he was asking for trouble. Musically, the piece is already risky enough: it involves a number of unusual sound effects (a train whistle, a siren, the stamp of marching feet) and a wider-than-average collection of instruments in the orchestra (including, for this performance, the Berlin Police Department's brass band and eight or nine accordion players). But what brought about the reaction in Berlin were the words of the cantata. Sung in Russian by a chorus of nearly a hundred and projected onto the proscenium arch in large German supertitles, these verses emphatically and repeatedly celebrated the Bolshevik Revolution, the birth of Communism, the triumph of the workers, etc., etc. At one point a man dressed up as Lenin came out onto the stage and harangued the audience with Lenin-style gestures, an intrusion that was clearly built into the score. All this was a bit more than certain elements of the Berlin audience could tolerate. For these former East and West Germans now attending a performance in what had once been West Berlin—as well as for the many Russians who had recently immigrated to the city, and who were probably represented at this Maryinsky concert in larger than usual numbers—Communism was far from a dead issue. So when the last notes of the music had sounded, the intense applause that met the orchestra's undeniably impressive achievement was punctuated by loud, threatening boos, clearly aimed not at the quality of the performance but at the meaning of the cantata's words.

I had heard booing before in a theater, but I had never heard boos that were this loud or sustained. They were just this side of scary, especially since the applause sector responded by clapping even louder, which in turn caused the boos to intensify. Gergiev took his bows with a small, ironic smile on his face, and then he briefly left the stage.

When he returned, he brought Lenin with him—and the actor proceeded to acknowledge his curtain call with appropriately Leninesque arm gestures. The booing faction was so offended by this that there was a momentary pause, as if for an intake of affronted breath, and then the boos came back louder than ever, as did the applause, which refused to die down until the booing was over. It was thrilling to hear music taken this seriously, and I had the sense that nowhere else in the world would the Prokofiev have created quite that response: this was musical history brought vigorously to life, so that the piece referred to its precise moment of performance as much as to its origins. That the objection had been purely political was confirmed at the end of the concert's second half, when the final notes of the astonishing (and astonishingly well played) Shostakovich symphony were greeted by a long, reverential silence, and then by thunderous applause on the part of the whole audience, including the first-act naysayers.

I was not, before I went to Berlin, a particularly musical person. Like most people of my age and class, I had learned to play an instrument as a child (in my case it was the violin), but I had not been very good at it, and the minute I stopped playing, at the age of thirteen or so, I forgot how to read a score. As an adult, I became interested in opera, but I tended to come at it from the theatrical rather than the musical side. I am fond of saying about myself that I do not have a non-narrative bone in my body, and opera fed this side of me, though it's true that with composers I truly loved, like Rossini, I would buy and listen to the recordings at home without having a clue about what was happening in the plot. I also went to a fair number of concerts and enjoyed them amateurishly.

But my real access to music is and has always been through dance. I cannot, in general, remember melodic passages, but if I have seen a dance performed to a piece of music, those particular passages stay with me; and whereas I remain utterly ignorant about most aspects of music theory, I can parse the rhythm of a musical piece almost instinctively. Much of my feeling for music can be traced back to my favorite choreographer, Mark Morris, whose own musicality is his most commonly noted attribute. A number of the recordings I have bought over the years are pieces I was first exposed to through his dances, and even my growing interest in vocal music can perhaps be traced to his affection for the human voice. But this becomes one of those chicken-and-egg questions, for in order to fall instantly under Mark Morris's spell, as I did when I first saw his work, I must have had *some* musical sensibility on which he could begin to build. In any case, the ear I brought with me to Berlin had been trained by Morris's choreography to be receptive, even if it had been trained in very little else.

During the several months I was in Berlin, I went to an average of three musical performances a week; some weeks I even went to five or six. This was not only because the quality was so high (though it almost always was), nor just that the tickets were so inexpensive (though government subsidies insured that they were: you could regularly get a good seat at the opera for less than a quarter of what it would have cost in San Francisco or New York). Part of the reason I took to Berlin's music so avidly was that it seemed so closely bound up with the life of the city. All sorts of people listened to live classical music in Berlin: students in jeans, provincial women dressed up in dirndl-like outfits, foreigners, locals, people with money, people without. (There was even one homeless-looking man—an American, I thought, judging by the one time I heard him speak—who showed up at most of the concerts I did and seemed always to get in at the last minute for free.) Nor was concert attendance just a form of display or recreation, as it so often seems in

American cities. These Berliners knew their stuff, and they weren't shy about expressing their response to the performances. You could learn a lot about musical performance standards just by sitting among them.

They knew how to be silent, too, which is at least as important an attribute in an audience. I remember the first concert I heard in the Berlin Philharmonic hall, an auditorium ingeniously designed to convey the softest notes, the loudest chords, and every shade of volume in between. Sitting there waiting for the Brahms Requiem to begin, I realized that I had never heard precisely that quality of silence before—a silence that was a combination of audience attentiveness and acoustical perfection.

In order to attend this particular Brahms concert (which wasn't even performed by the fabled Philharmonic orchestra itself, just a visiting group from Stuttgart), I had to forgo a much-praised performance of *La Traviata* at the Staatsoper that night. I also had to overcome my initial distaste for the Berliner Philharmoniker building, with its scaly gold-toned skin glinting in the trafficky mess near Potsdamer Platz. My idea, to the extent I can now reconstruct it, was that I would try the venue just once, and then confine myself as much as possible to the more attractive neighborhood around the

Staatsoper and the Konzerthaus, an area that East Germany had fortunately been too poor to remodel.

But, as so often when one quells an initial and largely imaginary aversion, I was to become hopelessly smitten with the Philharmoniker, so that even its local S-Bahn station—a vast space containing an as-yet-unfinished train line, complete with pristine white staircases and untraveled tracks, which always reminded me of a Fritz Lang set—came to seem welcoming and attractive because of its pleasurable associations. I was to become addicted, in particular, to Simon Rattle's performances, so that I began to refuse to leave town, even for a weekend, if I knew that one of his Philharmonic concerts was coming up. My husband, attempting to budge me from this position, pointed out that I would be missing an infinite number of performances after we left Berlin, so I had better learn to live with this condition; but, as with all such attempts to dissuade addicts, this only made me cling more insistently to my precious Philharmonic tickets.

On this first occasion, though, it was the auditorium rather than the conductor or the orchestra that won me over. As I sat in my cheap but excellent seat, feeling the waves of the *German Requiem* reverberate through my body and basking in the cunningly designed intimacy of the Philharmonic hall, I understood (or perhaps it would be more accurate to say "believed," since only time will prove the truth of this perception) that music had suddenly gained a new importance in my life, and that I myself had become a slightly different person as a result.

Nor did the magic end when I left the concert hall. Joining the crowd of satisfied audience members at the bus stop just outside the Philharmonic's front door, I surged with them aboard the overstuffed Number 200 bus that bore us convivially to Zoo Station. There I mounted the not-yet-familiar steps that led to the Potsdam-bound regional express platform and waited about five minutes for the train to pull in. When it did, I saw through the lighted windows of the nearest compartment my *Traviata*-going friends, who had just boarded the express at Friedrichstrasse at the end of *their* evening's performance. So natural did this seem, so consistent with the *Midsummer-Night's-Dream*-like nature of my newly acquired musical attentiveness, that I barely registered surprise at the happy coincidence. My friends, too, seemed shockingly unshocked by my sudden reappearance in their midst; all they wanted to do was tell me how wonderful the opera had been, just as I only wanted to babble away at them about the Brahms Requiem.

That experience encapsulated, for me, one of the things that made Berlin so special: its weird and unpredictable combination of smalltown intimacy with worldclass sophistication. The smalltownishness verged on the absurd. My husband and I could hardly go out on a Saturday night, in this city of over three million people, without running into someone we knew—and we only knew about thirty other people in town. The city seemed strangely underpopulated (actually, it *is* underpopulated, compared with its pre-war self), and as a result we could almost always get a ticket to any event we wanted to attend. Yet these events, which ranged from operas to concerts to strange, hybrid forms (like a grippingly theatrical all-male *Così fan tutte,* performed to piano music for four hands, that we saw in a little upstairs cabaret theater on Neukölln's Karl Marx Strasse), were consistently better than anything we would have been likely to see had we gone out three nights a week in London or Paris. And then, when we came out of these performances, there was none of the usual searching around for a place to eat—everything in Berlin stayed open late, and opened up early too, and remained open all through the day, so that one could conceivably spend from eleven a.m. to three a.m. in the same bistro—and at the end of the evening there was always a middle-of-the-night train you could catch to get home. All this seemed to mark Berlin as the most worldly and cosmopolitan kind of city. And yet it had none of the ingrained snobbishness or annoying self-esteem of most other capital cities. It somehow knew that it was just a jumped-up small town, at heart, and it made a virtue of the fact.

I often heard people say—my friend Martin among them—that Berlin was basically a proletarian town. A proletarian town that contained three major opera companies, the world's best orchestra, and an incomparable art collection divided up among dozens of museums struck me as a rather humorous oxymoron, to say the least. But that was only because I was used to England and America, where art and culture were inextricably bound up with private money. In Germany, the state paid for all this, or a great deal of it, and the things I had been brought up to view as costly if essential luxuries were just plain essentials in Berlin. It was as if I had gone to sleep and woken up in some kind of socialist dream, but without the unpleasant appurtenances that socialist dreams often carry with them.

And I did see what people meant about the proletarian character of the city. It was not just that Berlin lacked any hereditary aristocracy or any sizable class of successful businesspeople, though this was indeed true, but that these notable absences gave rise to a whole set of urban attitudes unlike anything I had ever seen in a metropolis before. There was none of that looking over one's shoulder to see how well or poorly everyone else was doing, and there was none of that desperate competition for scarce luxuries—these being two of the defining characteristics of New York, say, with which Berlin is otherwise often compared. On the contrary, the notion of luxury or competition had almost no meaning in Berlin. There were one or two restaurants where it might be a little difficult to get an immediate reservation, but if you waited a few days the problem went away, and in any case no one cared about restaurants in Berlin. That was part of what made it a proletarian town.

This aspect of Berlin perhaps became clearest to me the night I attended the Rem Koolhaas opening at the Neue Nationalgalerie. Because, as an architect, Koolhaas couldn't help but feel competitive with the marvelous Mies van der Rohe building in which his show was to take place, he had obtained special permission to stage the exhibit on the upper, glass-walled floor of the gallery, a huge space which is almost always left empty. In the event, this proved to be a disastrous aesthetic decision— both Mies's and Koolhaas's architecture looked the worse for it—but in prospect it had a terrific lure, and the opening party for the Koolhaas show was the hottest ticket in town. Or would have been, rather, if the opening had

taken place in New York, where only the richest and arti-
est and most beautiful of the city's elite would have been
allowed to attend. In Berlin, anyone who knew anyone
who had ever had anything to do with the arts could get
in; in fact, I don't think a single gate-crasher was turned
away, despite the pretense at an invitation list. Nor did the
guests resemble the usual New York *crème de la crème*.
There were a large number of extremely scruffy architecture students, for instance, who spent most of the party
sitting together on the floor of the museum's lower level,
guzzling the free beer and chatting with their equally
scruffy friends. Then there were the milling crowds of
gawkers on the exhibition floor itself, none of whom displayed the bare minimum of fashion sense that would be
required to walk safely down a Paris street. (Fashion, in
general, is not something that has infiltrated Berlin. That
too is part of what it means to be a proletarian town.)
Some of the guests may well have been socially important people, but it was impossible to tell who they might
be—they were all swirled together in the crowd, the
important and the unimportant, with Rem Koolhaas in
their midst, his tall, beaky profile only occasionally visible
over the mass of heads.

The Koolhaas opening wasn't the only place I encountered this raw, bracingly unrefined excitement. As a

matter of fact, I saw a version of it every time I went to any kind of contemporary art event, even in those cases where the art wasn't particularly good. There is something about Berlin that allows it to combine its own brand of world-weary pessimism with a perennially youthful sense of enthusiasm, and this in turn means that a certain kind of naivety—a quality which one needs in order to constantly reinvent the arts for one's own generation—is available in Berlin in a form that is neither false nor stupid. It is a richly inflected innocence, a zeal for the new that is premised on both appreciation of and wariness about the old. We have nothing like it in America. Every few years New York (and then the rest of the country) goes into a tortured soul-search and decides that we are all too ironic, that irony must now be thrown out so that something more—more what? more childlike? more authentic? more credulous?—something fresher and newer, at any rate, can be ushered in. But you cannot will such reforms, and in any case the thing that substitutes for irony, in America, is almost always worse than what it is replacing. In Berlin, on the other hand, there is no need to indulge in this kind of fruitless search for the uncorrupted, because the built-in German sense of bleakness (which lies deep within the culture, and which recent events have only confirmed) is able to coexist with a quite inspiring sense of optimistic inventiveness. The possibility that things are terrible does not obliterate the hope that they might also be great.

It is something I am always looking for, this intelligent innocence, this case-hardened optimism. I thought I had found it once before in my life, in another country, in another time. When I was twenty-one, I went to live in England for two years, and I fell madly in love with the place in very much the same way I was later to fall for Berlin. That too was a difficult time in American history (my English stay encompassed the late stages of the Vietnam War, the Watergate hearings, and the televised fiery deaths of the Symbionese Liberation Army, among other gruesome events), and so I was perhaps more prone than usual to admire anything that was not America. But England offered more than this. It was a place that seemed to have left its glory days behind, and in the aftermath of empire it displayed what struck me as a certain becoming modesty.

Success, in the England of that time, was seen as something brash and superficial, while honorable failure had its articulate adherents. The subtle and complex—whether in art, in politics, or in daily speech—took precedence over the easy and the obvious. Wisdom was more highly valued than information, but even information came in an appealing form: Penguin and Puffin books were cheap and attractive, the best British newspapers of that day were far more thoughtful and comprehensive than the *New York Times,* and the BBC made even television and radio into something smart and interesting. And while the life of the mind was acknowledged, so were the needs of the hungry body—not so much by the food per se (which was almost uniformly terrible, in the then-typical British manner) but through the overriding concern for public welfare. The Labor Party was still unflinchingly socialist in its aims, and most important functions were either state-run or state-subsidized. This included the arts, which flourished at a very high level: theater, literature, music, and sculpture offered the most outstanding examples, but the new National Film Theatre was also terrific, as was the Royal Ballet. And all of this—reading matter, medical care, films and plays, higher education, pub lunches, even rental housing— was affordable by almost anyone.

Margaret Thatcher changed all this. She didn't act alone, of course: history, in the form of Ronald Reagan, Rubert Murdoch, and other destroyers of the public good, helped her out. I was shocked to see how completely an entire country could alter its basic nature, how quickly things that had once seemed permanent could disappear. Within less than a generation, Britain went from having the best newspapers in English to having the worst; a nation that had once been singularly decent and polite turned into a hive of ruthless rudeness; and daily life in London became more frenzied, more superficial, and more money-oriented than anything one normally saw in New York.

So when I once again came across this dream, thirty years later in Berlin, I understood exactly how fragile it was. If anything, the commitment to the arts, the level of public education, and the connection between individual and common benefit seemed even deeper in Germany than they had in England. Lengthy newspaper commentaries on the latest opera production or political development, written by knowledgeable people with enormous space at their disposal, were a routine part of the German press, and it seemed impossible to imagine that these features, which the German readership took for granted, could ever disappear. But I knew that a mere decade or two of bottom-line business practices could wipe them out. Even while I was there, highly placed politicians and economists were talking about how the subsidies to the arts might have to be cut, in order to address Berlin's parlous financial condition. When I pointed out that the arts were exactly what could draw paying customers to the city, my native informants told me, yes, well, *we* know that, but try telling it to the legislators and the bookkeepers. In any case, I was ambivalent about the idea of drawing people to the city at all. Berlin's pleasing uncrowdedness—the fact that it had not yet been discovered by tourists, so that you could stand for half an hour in the Vermeer room of the Gemäldegalerie without being interrupted by another soul—was part of what made me love the place. As with the London of the 1970s, Berlin's poverty was a significant aspect of its virtue, and I was loath to see it disappear. In my (admittedly limited) experience of Western cities, humane impecuniousness is too often replaced by ill-divided wealth, so that what seems an overall improvement is actually, for most people, a tangible loss. It was this fate, which had overtaken all the other cities I'd ever loved, that I most feared for Berlin.

I could see for myself that the daily German papers contained long, erudite articles on politics and the arts, but I couldn't actually *read* any of them, because my German was almost non-existent. This, at the beginning, posed less of a problem than you might imagine. To an English speaker, German is an inherently welcoming language.

It's partly that so many of the words sound the same, and it's also a matter of grammatical resemblance. When I asked my German teacher, for instance, how to say "Can I sit here?" (useful for those moments on the train when a package was taking up a seat), she gave me "Kann ich hier sitzen?" while also alerting me to the fact that—just as in English—a stickler might quibble with the substitution of "can" for "may." This superficial similarity between the languages gave me the illusion, at first, that I was picking up German very rapidly. And the Germans colluded in this self-deception of mine. At ticket offices or local shops, in cafés or museums, the Berliners I dealt with were always happy to act as if my bits and pieces of the language were functional markers; they would accept them as good currency and reply in kind. It was only when I ran out of my meager supply and had to resort to the inevitable "Wie sagt man in Deutsch . . . ?" (How do you say in German . . . ?) that the whole artificiality of the game would be revealed. For their English was always so much richer than my German that they could invariably supply the missing word, gracefully translating the English one I had given them into the language we then continued to pretend to speak.

Thinking back on it now, I realize that I had one earlier exposure to the German language which foreshadowed my sudden enthusiasm in Berlin. Sometime in the early years of *The Threepenny Review*—which means more than fifteen or twenty years ago, now—the magazine acquired a German-language essay about the musician Tom Waits. A fluent German speaker produced a first-round translation for me; then I took home both versions, the English and the German, and began to tinker. With nothing but a German-English dictionary and a native sense of English idiom to guide me, I worked late into the night at my glass-topped dining room table. It is a table I still own (though it now occupies the dining room of a different house): its rectangle of extra-strength glass originally belonged to a friend, who had had it cut for an office doorway that it then failed to fit; my friend, knowing I wanted a glass-topped table, gave me the orphaned piece and referred me to an architect, who worked for weeks at this brain-teaser of a project, constructing panels and plugs to fit the pre-cut holes in the door. Finally he presented me with a unique and beautiful object. "How much do I owe you?" I asked. "You can't pay me what you owe me," the architect answered, "but I'm going to charge you the six hundred dollars we agreed on."

I don't know why I tell this story now, except that the expenditure of the architect's time on the table and mine on the German essay seemed to bear some relation to each other. What I mainly remember is how immensely satisfying the work was, how much pleasure I got from coming up with exactly the right corresponding terms for the German words I did not know but faintly apprehended. I felt—as I have never felt with Spanish, a language I know much better—that for once I understood the allure of translation. But I now think it was German rather than translation that appealed to me, because I felt the same thing again when I began to try to unpack the cunningly nested syllables I found all over Berlin.

This interpretive zeal, however, only took me a certain distance. Well before the end of my several months' stay, I had run up against the obdurate difficulty of the language: its irregular verbs, its masculine, feminine, and neuter articles, and above all its cases. I couldn't even understand *when* to use the genitive or the accusative, much less remember what forms they took. Nor could I read the simplest newspaper article (unless it was on a subject with which I was already familiar) or understand the most casual cocktail-party conversation. Forget Goethe and Kafka; I was halted at the language's outermost gates.

The fact that I was excluded from its linguistic recesses did not make me love Berlin any the less. On the contrary, my ignorance may well have shielded me and made me even more fondly doting. In England, I could almost always tell what was going on, and this had made me wary of the culture as well as attached to it. (The ads that lined the escalators in the Underground were always a particular object of my ire: even when I most loved London, my reaction to those ads hinted to me that I could also come to hate it.) Whereas, in Berlin, I could pretty much perceive only what I wanted to perceive. Other people would tell me about the outbreaks of anti-Semitic rage in the hinterlands or the mistreatment of Turks in the cities, but I couldn't read about these things for myself, so my experience of them was always attenuated, indirect, known but not fully felt.

At the same time, my sense of helplessness about the German language brought me weirdly closer to the German character, because it lent my time in Berlin an air of melancholy that is otherwise foreign to my nature. I became, in that sense, more German, less American. I do not think of myself, normally, as being very American, but I have in my make-up certain qualities that are frequently associated with my native place—a vast fund of energy, for one thing, and a correspondingly deep well of optimism and self-confidence. I am not used to thinking that there are things beyond my powers. But Berlin made me aware of my shortcomings: not only my inability to speak German, but also my ignorance about music, my insufficient grasp of history, my careless approach to scholarship, my amateurish way of looking at paintings . . .

Yet it would be wrong to suggest that these discoveries of my own inadequacies only disheartened me. They also freed me, in some way, to be something other than I had always been. Berlin—and the American Academy in particular, where I was cosseted, cared for, given no responsibilities and no onerous tasks—created the equivalent of an asylum room or a mother's lap, a place where I was protected enough to risk feeling loss and sorrow. So when I stood outside the Wannsee Conference House and imagined I was sensing Hitler's evil, that may not have been at all what I was really apprehending. Perhaps what I felt then was only my own stored-up melancholy, the suppressed sadnesses of a lifelong optimist, which Berlin seemed strangely and uniquely designed to release.

I had specific things to be sad about in that fall of 2003. My old friend Lenny had died the previous May, and my only son had gone away to college in August. I don't know how I would have handled these losses in the course of my regular life, if I had not gone to Berlin—no doubt by tamping them down, ignoring them as much as possible, keeping a stiff upper lip. (It was not for nothing, that affinity I had felt with England in my youth.) I do not mean to suggest that my sorrows were huge or unbearable: they were normal human sorrows, and tiny relative to many others. But that comparative, ameliorating mode, which is so easy for an American to fall into, is not always the best approach even to normal-sized sorrows. It is possible, I now realize, to face sadness without falling into self-pity or depression, and it is possible to submit to melancholy without becoming completely incapacitated. This is something I did not know before I went to Berlin.

The self that I took with me to Berlin was both continuous with and slightly altered from the self I had lived with for my previous fifty-one years. Montaigne would say this was true of any self, at any age, but I felt it particularly strongly at that point. I was at a juncture of some sort. I wanted to leave things behind, my own personality included—and yet, since I clearly could not do that (and just as clearly did not wish to, at least on some level), I also wanted to take a long, intense, self-possessed but not possessive look at my life, and the world, and my history in relation to the world's history. For reasons only partially connected with my age, the idea of death, and particularly my own death, had recently become far less abstract to me, and I wanted the time to think about that. Germany was a good place to have such thoughts, or at any rate a better place for them than I'd ever encountered before. Perhaps there is indeed something behind these spurious notions of a national character— notions that at their worst produce a Hitler, and at their best produce most of the novels I've ever cared for.

In February of 2003, seven months before I set off for Berlin, I saw an exhibition of photographs by a German photographer, Thomas Struth, at the Metropolitan Museum in New York. I had never heard of him before, but the best of his pictures—huge color photos that showed artworks in museums, with people standing in front of them and looking at them—moved me as few photographs ever have. Partly this was because Struth's choice of artworks (Caillebotte's *Paris Street; Rainy Day,* Delacroix's *Liberty Guiding the People,* a Vermeer from the National Gallery in London, and so forth) included a number of paintings that have been unusually important to me. But it was also due to the fact that he had captured something alive about the paintings, something that I would have called unreproducible if he had not, indeed, managed to reproduce it. What I saw, when he pointed it out to me, was the way people in an art museum could mirror—in their posture, in the color and cut of their clothing, in their physical relation to each other (even, in the case of the Vermeer, in their apparent absence from the room)—something essential in each painting, so that the artwork in front of them actually seemed to extend off the wall into their viewing space, and thence into ours. This feeling of the continuity between art and lived experience so permeated these photographs (I want to say "these paintings," for this is how the photos struck me, as paintings themselves) that it seemed useless to buy postcards or catalogues of Struth's work, and so I didn't. The only way to see them was as one sees a painting: life-sized on a wall.

A couple of days after seeing the photographs I saw Struth himself. He was appearing on a panel at the Goethe Institute, directly across the street from the exhibition of his photos. In a way that I did not then recognize but have since come to see as Berlin-like, the lecture room was filled with sloppily dressed, eager young people as well as the more sedate art-museum types one would expect on that stretch of Fifth Avenue. Struth himself, dressed in black and with close-cropped gray hair, was an engaging figure in early middle age who spoke excellent if accented English. Everything he said confirmed the sense I had of him from his photos, but what I remember best is the word he used to describe his relationship to the material. "I want to use the word 'submit,'" he said, "but without any sense of forced obedience or something like that. I want it to include free choice, and will, but also a sense of giving myself over to something, allowing myself to be taken over. But perhaps I have chosen the wrong word since my English is not so good."

Later, someone in the audience asked him if there was anything particularly German about his work. Struth was clearly uncomfortable with the question, and yet he wanted to give it an answer that justified its having been asked. "I don't usually think of myself as particularly German," he said. "It's a hard question to answer. But I guess I would say—yes, well, I love the music of Bach. And so I hope there is something in my photographs that is like Bach."

At the time I thought these were good answers, but now I feel they're even better. Because now that I have observed German culture in action, I understand something about the way it draws together seeming opposites. To submit oneself completely—to a moment of photographic time, to the feeling generated by a landscape or a city or a work of art—and yet to have the clarity, the precision, the control evident in a Bach composition: these are not only instructive endpoints in a possible spectrum, but actual and simultaneous options. I have heard them both at once in a Beethoven or Schubert piece at the Berliner Philharmoniker; I have seen them both in Caspar David Friedrich or Adolph Menzel paintings at the Alte Nationalgalerie. Before I went to Berlin, if I had thought about it at all, I would have thought about these two strands of German culture as entirely separate and opposed: there was the "feeling" strand expressed in German Romanticism, which risked sickly sweetness at its most extreme, and there was the "structure" strand expressed in Bach or the Bauhaus, which risked coldness at *its* extreme. But of course Bach's music contains tremendous feeling—the form, the clarity, are themselves expressive, just as they are in Struth's most formally satisfying photos and Friedrich's most formally perfect paintings. The sweetness in each is mediated by the coldness, and vice versa. The risks are thus disarmed, but only because they have both been submitted to.

Mittelweg 36 is the name of the magazine my friend Martin edits. When he first gave me his business card, he explained that the publication was only called that because it was the street address at which the magazine's offices happened to be located. But later I started to think about this. How could a leftwing magazine innocently be called "middle way"? Didn't this hint at Clintonian or Blairish political compromise, with its craven attempt to reach the voters in the center? Wasn't it disingenuous to say that the title had no meaning?

When I confronted Martin with these thoughts, he said, "Ah, but in German the phrase has a different association. If you ask most German people what they think of when you say *Mittelweg*, they will quote you the proverb *In Gefahr und grösster Not bringt der Mittelweg den Tod*." I couldn't follow the spoken German, but Martin's wife Barbara, a professional translator, immediately rendered it into English for me: "In situations of danger and greatest distress, the middle course will bring death." In other words, you must take sides, choose one thing or another, go for the extremes. If you are unable to choose—if you opt instead for the wishy-washy-ness of the middle—you will end up with nothing. There is a slightly scary willfulness to this attitude (especially given the extremities of Germany's recent history), but there is also something admirably dark and bravely hard-edged about it, and I found myself instantly attracted to the saying, not least because it seemed so deeply un-American.

We, with our cautious "Look before you leap" and our nervous "A bird in the hand is worth two in the bush"—what do we know of the Mittelweg that is death? And how far can we ever expect to get without that knowledge?

Certain places are capable of becoming significant to us only at certain times—I mean not only at particular phases of their own history, but at particular moments in ours. I was ready for Berlin when I finally got to it. There are always dissatisfactions and longings that arise with middle age, feelings about roads not taken and opportunities missed. Berlin was both the spur and the antidote to these feelings in me. It made me want to become something other than what I had been before, but it also made me recognize the futility of that desire, and in the end it also made me able to live peaceably, if not happily, with that futility. Being in Berlin allowed me, possibly for the first time in my life, to experience regret.

It would be something of an understatement to say that regret has never been much of a factor in my psychological make-up. This is true on the daily level as well as over the long haul. I make decisions quickly and easily, and I rarely second-guess myself. If there is a possible mistake looming in the future, I anxiously do my best to avoid it, but if an unrectifiable mistake has already occurred, I can pretty quickly let it go. I do not, as a rule, look back on any moments of my past and say, "Here is where the determining choice was made, and here is where I went wrong." I am deeply attached to novels that contain such moments, but I do not seem to find them echoed in my own life. For the most part, the path behind me looks like a straight, clear road from this end: things seem to have turned out, for me, the way I should have expected them to turn out, if I had ever bothered to imagine the future, which I pretty rigorously did not. I am not saying this hindsight is accurate. There were probably many alternative branches that have been lost in the mists of oblivion, if not obliviousness. But I have been protected from thinking about or even knowing about these alternatives by my tendency to keep my head down and just keep plowing forward. This behavior was not just a matter of smug self-satisfaction or crude lack of imagination; it was also the result, I now think, of fear. I suspect I was afraid that if regret once got a foot in the door, it might succeed in bringing down the whole structure.

Berlin somehow got round that fear, and in doing so it made me able to picture the possibility of another life: not one I could have had if I had chosen differently, but one that would have required me to be a completely different person. The Berlin I would have wanted to inhabit, when I was in my twenties or thirties, did not exist when I was in my twenties or thirties, and neither did the person who would have wanted to inhabit it. I have only reached that stage now. I am only now—through the collaboration of all the forces, both personal and historical, that made me what I became over the last fifty years—the kind of person who can appreciate Berlin for what *it* is now, in all its complicated self-dividedness. And yet I am too old to start over again. That, I imagine, is what all the middle-aged Jews said when they contemplated leaving Berlin for America in the 1930s, though in their case the consequences of the choice were far more dire. I do not have history breathing down my neck (except insofar as the America of the early twenty-first century is somewhere one might want to get away from). I can afford to say, "I am too old to learn a new language, I am too old to give up my house and my friends, I will stay where I am." I can live with that decision, and live well.

But it is sad to feel that one is too old, even for things one doesn't really need. It is a feeling that middle-aged Americans don't easily embrace, especially *this* middle-aged American, who has spent a lifetime avoiding regrets. It seems that Berlin, in making me want something I cannot have—in making me want to *be* something I am not—has infected me with its own characteristic melancholy. I can struggle against the resignation. I can try to learn German, or take music lessons, or do any number of things to cement the connection between the person I briefly became in Berlin and the person I will be for the rest of my life. The struggle is no doubt salubrious, in that it is good to try new things, good to have doubts about the perfection of one's own existence. Still, it is hard for me to acknowledge the sad truth that I will never be a Berliner. Or, if I am a *sort* of Berliner, it is only in this way: that I have become permanently aware of a division in myself, between the person I might have become had I lived in Berlin, and the person I am instead.

Part Two

ON NOT WRITING
ABOUT DAVID HUME

There is always something sad about a book that doesn't see the light of day. It has about it the ghostly, lurid, frightening quality of those formaldehyde-filled jars of deformed fetuses and other anatomical grotesqueries that one sees in old movies about mad scientists. It reeks of the unborn and the undead, inhabiting that shadowy middle ground between things that actually exist and things that were never conceived of. Failure, hopelessness, and even a kind of shame cling to its unseen pages. This can be true even of a book that has been fully written but lives its entire life in an author's desk drawer. In that case, though, there is always the possibility that a resurrection may still take place: after the author dies, or even before, the manuscript pages may escape from their coffin and be transmuted into the bound pages of a published volume. But if the book has never even been written, there is no hope for it at all.

I had such a book; or perhaps I should say I have it still, for the book that never gets written never gets finished, either. Mine was, or is, about the philosopher David Hume.

When I first announced to my editor—a man who was himself trained in philosophy, though he has long since put it aside—that I wanted to write a short, lively, accessible critical biography of Hume, his response was surprisingly enthusiastic. My editor seemed to understand exactly why I found Hume so congenial. He also felt (or perhaps it was I who felt, with his tacit agreement) that Hume's time had come at last: his philosophical ideas were ripe for application to the world we now inhabit, and their humane, intelligent usefulness might even appeal to the general reading public. We were going to call the book *A Philosopher for Our Time,* or possibly *Hume Our Contemporary,* and while neither of us thought it would necessarily make any money, we both viewed it as a worthy project.

Simply having discussed the book in this way made me feel that I had practically written it—at any rate, that it was well on its way toward being a book. I am not the sort of writer or indeed the sort of person who has a lot of unfinished projects lying around, and I am generally very quick (sometimes, perhaps, too quick) to bring my projects to completion. So it seemed only a matter of time, once I had had this discussion, before the little critical biography would be out. Filled with the sense of purpose that always accompanies these beginning stages, I rushed out to buy as many books by and about David Hume as I could affordably lay hands on.

I already had quite a few David Hume books sitting on my shelves—mainly those little yellow paperbacks put out by Bobbs-Merrill, like *David Hume: Philosophical Historian* or *Of the Standard of Taste and Other Essays,* but also random volumes from the *Treatise of Human Nature* and the *Enquiries.* These volumes had all been acquired more than a quarter of a century earlier when I first encountered Hume, initially and briefly in two college courses, and then more seriously during a Cambridge term spent studying "Moralists" (that being the word the Leavis-influenced Cambridge English faculty used to refer to its Tripos exam in philosophy). The philosophers covered ranged from Aristotle to Freud. My tutor, John Casey, was widely known for his eccentric conservatism and his staunch misogyny, but neither of these qualities interfered with our tutorials, during which we engaged in lively debates about Aristotle's concept of the great man, Kant's categorical imperative, and other light-hearted topics.

Alone among the philosophers we read, Hume instantly struck me as a kindred figure, someone to be carried through life as a sort of talisman against non-sense. He was so specific, so visceral in his approach, that

I found myself drawn to his examples and thought processes even when I wanted to argue with them. I remember, for instance, being in the midst of the cold, gray, landlocked Cambridge winter and happening upon Hume's assertion that one cannot be proud of the Pacific Ocean (because pride entails possession, or at least intimate connection, and no one, obviously, can own the Pacific Ocean). A Californian in exile, I responded to these words with a rush of feeling for the Pacific Ocean, a sudden sense of how much I missed its western-facing sunsets, its tide-pooled shores inhabited by sea lions and sea otters, even its dangerous rocks and undertows. If this was not pride, it was as close to it as I could imagine feeling, and I was grateful to Hume for the evocative experience, even if it seemed to contradict the point he was trying to make.

I barely read a word of Hume after 1975, but somehow I retained a sense that he was *my* philosopher (rather in the way the Pacific Ocean was *my* ocean), a vast reserve on whom I could draw for sustenance as needed. He represented, for me, a common-sense view of the world, a down-to-earth answer to lofty abstractions, an adherence to the tangible and the everyday. It did not hurt that he was Scottish, since Edinburgh was one of the first European cities I had ever lived in, and the first I had fallen in love with. Best of all, Hume was an agnostic, or possibly even an atheist—at any rate, an anti-religious figure whose philosophy dispensed entirely with the need for a God.

This last is actually what brought me back to him in 2002. I can remember the moment exactly. I was sitting in the audience of the San Francisco Opera's production of *Saint François d'Assise,* the American premiere of Olivier Messiaen's starkly religious masterwork. It was a much-heralded, much-praised opera, and even I could see that it was very well done. But I was not enjoying myself. It was not just the music's unyielding modernism that put me off; though it's true that I'm a Handel/Rossini kind of person, I can easily be won over by a good performance of, say, Berg's *Lulu.* What made me so distinctly uncomfortable, in this case, was the life-defying religious sensibility that suffused the piece. The St. Francis who lived in my imagination (put there, no doubt, by his associations with my local metropolis) was a rather pleasant fellow who liked animals, but Messiaen's version was a much more ascetic figure, an aspiring martyr who wanted to feel pain, a man who longed to suffer agonies comparable to the crucifixion so he could prove and intensify his love of God. I felt innately antagonistic to this whole distaste-for-the-body routine, and as

I cast about for an alternative mode of thought (the opera was five hours long and sometimes the notes were few and far between, so there was a lot of room for alternative modes of thought), I recalled the pleasure-loving, rational-minded David Hume. It was at that moment that I decided to write a book about him.

Philosophers of intentionality have argued over whether the verb "decided to" can be used about an action that did not reach completion. *If you didn't carry through on the decision, then you didn't really decide to do it* was Gilbert Ryle's line—not in so many words, but that's what he meant, with his disparaging remarks about ghost-in-the-machine dualism and phantom actions. But Bernard Williams begged to disagree. There's a wonderful passage in his *Shame and Necessity* where he talks about a man who "decides" to abandon his mistress and go back to his wife, and then finds he can't live with that decision. Did he decide, or not? Bernard's worldview was subtle enough, and his experience of such moments visceral enough, that he could see the ambiguities in the situation; to his mind, it was possible to arrive at a decision that was invisible to an external observer and that resulted in no tangible outcome. I did, in that sense, decide to write a book about David Hume. Perhaps more to the point, I never decided *not* to write it. It's just that the book failed, over time, to emerge.

But the word "failed" makes the process sound too flaccid, too inactive and weak. I grappled, over the years, with this not writing about David Hume. Wherever I went, I would ship a boxload of Hume books—or, if it made more sense, check ten or twelve of them out on long-term loan from the local university library. Not writing about David Hume required the presence of David Hume books on my shelves: they had to be in clear view, overseeing the process of my not writing. Sometimes I even read them, or read in them, to rediscover what I was not writing about.

If you have ever come across a book by Geoff Dyer called *Out of Sheer Rage,* you will perhaps detect something familiar in my methodology. One of Dyer's two most brilliant books (the other, I think, is his recent one about photography), *Out of Sheer Rage* is about not writing about D. H. Lawrence. Dyer, too, schleps his research materials from country to country, only to find himself not using them. He too has a deep affinity with his subject and nothing much to show for it (except a few piercing paragraphs, scattered here and there within the book, that say more about Lawrence than most of the rest of the critical literature combined). And he too can't quite bear just to let the project go.

But Geoff Dyer and I are very different sorts of writers, and our ways of not doing something couldn't be more unlike. He specializes in torpor, in passive avoidance, in laziness carried to excess. Lying in bed reading *Out of Sheer Rage* (I was suffering from back problems at the time), I found his description of an average "writing" day—most of it spent lounging around in his bathrobe, occasionally in front of the TV—so oppressively convincing that I had to crawl out of bed and pay a few bills, just to make sure the contagion hadn't affected me. My own tendency in the avoidance department is to err on the side of frenzy and over-exertion. It is very easy for me to fill up my day with small, necessary, immediate tasks that prevent me from even thinking about David Hume, let alone writing about him. I would seem, in this sense, to be singularly unsuited to writing a book about a man who specialized in lengthy, quiet periods of thought and other sedentary enjoyments, such as eating, talking, and card-playing. Perhaps I would have done better to choose a more frenzied character, like D. H. Lawrence. And Geoff Dyer probably would have known better than I do how to grapple with David Hume's relative stillness.

I am speaking of Dyer-on-the-page, Dyer as he presents himself in his nonfiction books. When I eventually met Geoff Dyer, he turned out to be nothing like that narrator, or at least only sufficiently like him to prevent my having suspicions about plagiarism or ghost writing. I had learned that Dyer was to be in San Francisco, and so I had offered, sight unseen and purely on the basis of my affection for his writing, to take him out to lunch at the fanciest restaurant in my neighborhood. Then I had doubts. Would the boorish malcontent described in *Out of Sheer Rage* be able to sustain the decorum needed for a fancy restaurant? Would he even be able to sit up straight in his chair for as long as a lunch? In the event, these doubts proved groundless, for Geoff Dyer the person proved to be an attractive, well-spoken Englishman with impeccable restaurant manners. I should not have been surprised. The person and the writer are never exactly alike, even when the writing purports to be nonfiction.

Perhaps this is what began to worry me about my David Hume project as well. Which had I been attracted to, the person or the writer? Well, the writer, obviously—I knew very little about the person when I set out to do the book. But why, then, was I proposing to do a biography? And what possible light, in any case, could a biographical study shed on the philosophical writing? Often, I can't even explain the connections between my own life and my own essays; how could I expect to do so for a total stranger who had lived over two hundred years earlier in a far-away place?

Actually, the far-away place was part of the appeal. I had hopes of visiting Edinburgh again. It would be a tax-deductible visit, possibly even a grant-subsidized visit, a journey that would be converted from a fanciful holiday jaunt to a necessary research trip by virtue of my David Hume book. My first trip to Edinburgh, at the age of twenty, had been for the ostensible purpose of doing research on the Scottish city planner Patrick Geddes, the subject of my undergraduate thesis. I had fond memories of sitting in the Guildhall Library reading manuscripts and typescripts from the Geddes archive, and even fonder memories of exploring the city's streets and byways, its stunning vistas and ancient closes, its parks and promenades, its classically rectangular New Town and medievally twisty Old Town, all jumbled together in one walkable, learnable, livable city. When I thought up my David Hume project, I must have imagined that somehow I could transport myself back to that youthful period of discovery. Even more crazily, I imagined that the Edinburgh I could visit in the twenty-first century and the one Hume had occupied in the eighteenth retained sufficient elements in common for me to glean some clues about how and why he had become the kind of philosopher he was.

Perhaps I am just not biographer material. *Real* biographers (most notably Richard Holmes) actually do this following-in-the-footsteps thing and make it work for them. But I know damn well that if I visited the plaque on the wall marking David Hume's last residence in the New Town, it would only make me feel more hopelessly inept at capturing either his personality or his ideas. Even reading the other biographies of him made me feel that way. The more I learned about David Hume, the less I could get any kind of handle on him.

The basic outline is clear enough. He was born in Edinburgh in 1711 and grew up at Ninewells, the family estate in Berwickshire; he died, also in Edinburgh, in 1776. In between he attended Edinburgh College as a teenager, wrote his first (and eventually most influential) book of philosophy before the age of twenty-six, and worked for a while as an aide to a high-ranking military figure, during which time he traveled extensively through Europe. Though Scotland was his home for most of his life, he spent brief periods in London and one longish interval in Paris, where he served as the official secretary to the British ambassador, and where his reputation as both a philosopher and a historian brought him numerous French admirers. He never married, but he had at least one intense flirtation, possibly more epistolary than actual, with a highly intelligent Frenchwoman of the *haut monde;* some sources also think he seduced one of the local Ninewells girls in his youth, but there is no firm evidence for that. He befriended or was befriended by Adam Smith, James Boswell, Jean-Jacques Rousseau, and other noteworthy figures of his time. He practiced surreptitious acts of charity throughout his life, often putting his own hard-earned money and reputation toward the support of needier writers, but without letting them know he was behind the helpful efforts. As a matter of principle (there had been a disagreement, and his strong recommendation had not been heeded), he gave up a comfortable position at the Edinburgh law library at a time when he very much needed the resources it provided; from that time on he lived mainly on his writing. His anti-clericalism made him a bit of a black sheep in certain Edinburgh circles, but his manners were so charming and his conversation so entertaining that even the stiff-necked Scottish Presbyterians broke down and invited him to their homes. He died without reneging on his lifelong agnosticism: when Boswell asked him on his deathbed if he did not *now* believe that a future state was possible, "He answered that it was possible that a piece of coal put upon a fire would not burn," and as to whether the thought of annihilation made him uneasy, "He said not the least; no more than the thought that he had not been, as Lucretius observes." Among his friends and acquaintances, the adjective that most frequently accompanied his name was "good."

I liked this man. He would be excellent company, I felt, and would repay all the close attention I was planning to give him. But even at this purely biographical phase—before I ever dared to crack open the horrendously dense and often self-contractictory philosophical essays—I could see that David Hume was not the coherent, consistent package he initially seemed to be. There was, for instance, that odd sentence attributed to his mother: "Our Davie's a fine good-natur'd cratur, but uncommon weak-minded." What could this possibly mean when applied to the most brilliant man of his generation, if not, indeed, his century? Did the family really fail to perceive his intelligence? Did they, in some perverse way, view all this book-reading and thought-experimenting and treatise-producing as some kind of fool's errand?

Or did the phrase "weak-minded" refer instead to Hume's mental fragility, his tendency to break down after too much work? There does seem to have been a breakdown of sorts in the early 1730s, just after a long, strenuous period spent developing the ideas that were to emerge in the *Treatise of Human Nature*. We have as evidence a letter he wrote in 1734 to a specialist in London, piteously (and anonymously) detailing his symptoms, which included a watery mouth, a slight rash, a surge in appetite, an unaccustomed laziness, an inability to read or think consecutively, and a constant vacillation between idle melancholy and nervous exhaustion. Hume recovered from this episode of his youth, but he was never quite the same person afterward: where he had once been lean, rawboned, and rather pale, he was now increasingly portly and inclined to a ruddy cheerfulness.

But perhaps *weak-minded* did not, in eighteenth-century Scotland, mean what we now take it to mean. Some Scottish commentators have suggested that what his mother actually said was "wake-minded," which in the local dialect may have signified that he was smart, quick, alight with intelligence. This is, after all, reported speech rather than writing, so it could well have been misheard. Or perhaps she used the phrase sardonically, ironically, as Scots—now as then—are so wont to do, implying the exact opposite of what was explicitly said. Or maybe she never spoke these words at all, and the sentence is just part of the cultural effluvia, the originary myth, that is bound to arise around the shadowy childhood of any subsequently prominent figure. From this distance, we have no way of discriminating among all the possibilities, no way of deciding which comes closest to the truth.

Seeking out the singular and everlasting truth is not, in any case, a project with which David Hume himself would have had much sympathy. He was, in that sense, the opposite of a Platonist or a Kantian (to the extent, I mean, that Kant himself was a Platonist). He did not believe that the Truth was somewhere "out there," located in supernatural territory and accessible to us only through otherworldly communications. He did not think of truth as a pre-existing, permanent, capitalized phenomenon at all. To Hume, it seemed clear that truths (and they were always multiple) arose under specific circumstances and applied to specific circumstances. One arrived at them only through observation: of oneself, of one's own thought processes, of the world around one, of the historical record.

Sense data are very important to Hume. In his philosophy, they are not disguises or illusions, as they are for Platonists, but the key to reality—or rather, they are reality itself. Hume understood that our access to things outside ourselves can only come by way of our individual perceptions, so that it would be erroneous, or at any rate simplistic, to draw a firm line between subjective and objective realities. When he first came up with this notion, it seemed frighteningly radical and skeptical, but Hume's insight eventually turned out to be as sound as science—indeed, to *be* science, as the twentieth-century work of Einstein and Heisenberg made clear.

Though I have always lacked any shred of scientific temperament, and still do, Hume's way of viewing things has come to seem more and more useful to me the longer I live. As a young woman, I craved absolute distinctions. Everything, with me, got divided into two opposite extremes. I believed, for example, that there were two ways of writing: from the outside, for public purposes like academia and journalism, and from the inside, for letters, poetry, and other private communications. I wanted to put facts in one camp and opinions in another—which is not to say that I didn't lean toward the opinion camp myself (I did, most vociferously), but that I wanted facts to be somehow clean, undebatable, and separate from the mind that conceived them. And yet I longed, at the same time, for a brand of moral philosophy that would be eternal and absolute, that would have the force of "my" opinions and the solidity of "their" facts. (If you were to put this in Hume's terms, you might say that I longed for *is* to imply *ought*.) Now, though, as the rigidities of youth have loosed their hold a bit, I find that Hume's more nuanced take on the world satisfies my need for certainty. It is not that there are no truths. It is not that we cannot call some things wrong and others right. It is just that our ability to do so depends on a purely human, specific, temporary set of perceptions—temporary, I mean, in the sense that *we* are temporary.

Maybe it was Hume's own weak-mindedness, his awareness of how unreliable our thought processes can be, that enabled him to come up with his philosophical . . . I was going to write "system," but the word is misleading, because part of what he did, as a writer as well as a thinker, was to break down huge taken-for-granted systems of thought into their contradictory parts. He did this with religion, he did it with history, and he did it with psychology and philosophy, which for him were completely intertwined subjects. Whether he was talking about aesthetics or science, ethics or epistemology, he was interested in the extremely specific mechanisms whereby one absorbs information and formulates ideas. He would not have been so interested in the way the mechanism worked, I think, had he not also been aware of how it could cease to work. He did not, that is, take perception for granted. His own ability to believe what his senses transmitted to him contained within it, and was ultimately strengthened by, his capacity for doubt.

David Hume was nothing if not sane, but he had an uncanny attraction to and for madness in others. I know people like this myself—attractive, extremely intelligent, often charismatic figures who give off some kind of aura that attracts lunatics. My friend Stephen, for instance, can barely take a medium-length trip without having the person in the seat next to him make some bizarre confession or issue some unreasonable demand; even those who look perfectly sane when they board the plane or train or bus seem compelled to reveal their innate nuttiness once they are seated next to Stephen. I do not mean to be New-Age-y about this. I am not saying that the lunatics can *see* Stephen's special aura. All I'm saying is that certain finely attuned sensibilities, particularly sensibilities that are themselves open to skepticism, doubt, and other fluid states, are more likely than others to engage the attention of the mad. David Hume seems to have been one of these people.

There was, for instance, his experience working as a tutor to a markedly deranged young aristocrat. He took the job at a moment of financial and personal desperation, a few years after the unsuccessful publication of his *Treatise* (which in his view had fallen *"dead-born from the Press"*) and just after he had been turned down for the Edinburgh Moral Philosophy Chair; he took it, that is, because he had to. But I think he also took it because he thought it would be relatively undemanding work. How much tutoring, after all, could a mad person require? The young Marquess of Annandale was in fact sane enough to invite David Hume to come live with him, but it was made clear to the new tutor, even at that initial stage, that restorative quiet had been prescribed in response to the youthful nobleman's symptoms of mental instability. Annandale already had an ongoing minder, in the form of his faithful valet, as well as various other servants and medical attendants on tap. Knowing this, Hume must have assumed that he was merely charged with having some pleasant literary conversations during the lucid intervals, and would otherwise be left pretty much on his own in the great country house. Or perhaps he was not fully informed of Lord Annandale's mental condition beforehand, and imagined he was simply occupying the role of a gentleman's companion. What could "tutor" mean in the case of a veritable grown-up, a man nearly Hume's own age?

What it meant, in the event, turned out to be a combination of babysitter, advocate, and desperate employee. Things started benignly enough: Annandale was a good fellow, despite his erratic behavior, and Hume grew quite fond of him. But then, as the weather and the household's finances declined, the young lord's condition worsened. At its depths, his illness sounded like psychosis of some kind, possibly schizophrenia; at less extreme moments it resembled manic-depression. (I am diagnosing after the fact, of course—Hume simply reported the symptoms.) Whatever else it included, Lord Annandale's condition definitely contained an element of paranoia.

Unfortunately, the paranoia was to a certain extent justified—as when is it not?—by the treatment the young lord was receiving at the hands of his official guardians. There was a mother somewhere, but she was apparently in thrall to the evil demon controlling Annandale's purse strings: that is, one "Captain Vincent" (or possibly just plain Mr. Vincent—the military title may well have been an affectation), who had apparently been instrumental in hiring David Hume, no doubt figuring that this penniless writer would be the perfect patsy. But Hume was not one to accept injustice silently or passively. He fired off a seemingly endless round of letters—to the nakedly self-serving Mr. Vincent, to a distant relative of Annandale's named Sir James Johnstone, and even to Annandale's otherwise invisible mother—trying to get Vincent dethroned. Faced with an absolute lack of cooperation, Hume threatened to leave before the end of his promised term, though he hated to abandon the pathetic young lord (and he also needed to collect his salary, which had not been forthcoming as promised). Annandale apparently wanted to be left alone—so, at any rate, he told Hume—and Hume was grudgingly willing to leave him, but not until he did his best to right the wrongs of the situation. Meanwhile, though, he was inhabiting an increasingly gloomy mansion with an increasingly loony and unhappy pupil—until, at the end of a full year, he simply gave up and fled.

You might think this was enough craziness to last Hume a lifetime, but the worst was still to come, for David Hume had yet to encounter Jean-Jacques Rousseau. That meeting between the great Scottish philosopher and the famous Swiss one took place in Paris in 1765, fully twenty years after the Annandale incident, by which time Hume had become the intimate of French aristocrats and the toast of French royalty, mainly on the basis of his multi-volume *History of England*. (There is a funny letter—Hume was a wonderful letter-writer, in that he knew how to make himself look both good and bad at the same time—in which he describes being praised by every member of the French royal family in turn, down to the toddling Prince, who "likewise advanced to me in order to make me his harangue, in which, though it was not very distinct, I heard him mumble the word *histoire,* and some other terms of panegyric.")

The first meeting between Hume and Rousseau was an occasion of profuse mutual flattery and sincere expressions of affection—sincere, at least, on Hume's part, and when did Rousseau ever understand himself well enough to be consciously insincere? In his usual generous manner, Hume had volunteered to help the impoverished, rebellious, persecuted hermit flee from France, where he was in danger of being arrested, and relocate safely in England. This alone turned out to be more of a task than Hume had reckoned on, since Rousseau insisted on bringing along his harridan of a mistress as well. And then, once he had been installed in a large house in the English countryside (a house borrowed from one of Hume's wealthier acquaintances), Rousseau began to turn against his benefactor. He declared that he was being mistreated, kept from his friends, deprived of all means of livelihood—and that the villain who perpetrated all these crimes against him was the dastardly David Hume.

Hume, meanwhile, who had already spent some of his own limited earnings on keeping the Rousseau household afloat, had begun to petition the King of England for a royal pension to support the refugee philosopher. And here is the nub of the tale, the twist that makes it so Humean. He *continued* to pursue the pension for Rousseau, vigorously and ultimately successfully, even as Rousseau was badmouthing him to anyone who would listen. At the same time, he lost patience with the man and eventually sent an open letter to the French papers, declaring his own innocence and denouncing Rousseau's attacks on him. For this, Hume was roundly criticized: people felt he should not have stooped to the public forum in resolving this personal dispute. The excuse he gave was that he had been pushed to the limit, not only by Rousseau's ingratitude, but by his own fear that his reputation would suffer as a result of Rousseau's lies.

But even at this point, in the midst of his anger and distress and shame, he went on trying to secure the royal pension. When it finally came through, Rousseau, who had repeatedly declared he would take no money that came to him through Hume's agency, nonetheless pocketed the money happily (or as happily as he ever did anything, which was not very). And Hume, though he never spoke to the ingrate again, kept for the rest of his life a pair of matching portraits that had been done of him and Rousseau by the Scottish painter Allan Ramsay; when he died, they were still hanging side by side on the wall of his Edinburgh flat.

Or so I remember the story. I have not looked back at all the various biographies and letters to see if I recalled every detail correctly, and in any case how would it matter if I did not? After all, I am not writing about David Hume.

He would have hated that cavalier tone about the facts. He was a historian as well as a philosopher, and even as a philosopher he was the kind who believed in details, in accuracy. (Isn't it odd how many of them do not? How, I always wonder, did they ever find their way into a line of work that advertises itself as searching for the truth?) Perhaps part of the reason I am avoiding writing about him is that I don't feel I can stand up to his scrupulous regard for the facts. As my historian friend Tom is always pointing out, facts have never been my strong point.

This is not to say that I am a liar. On the contrary, I seem to be one of the more naturally truthful people I know: not out of any sense of virtue, but simply out of lack of imagination, or inability to make up a lie quickly enough, or bullheaded disregard for the feelings of others, or some other factor which would explain my failure even to come up with unimportant or tactful lies at opportune moments. When a stranger asks my name, for instance—I mean a stranger on a train, someone I will never see again—it doesn't occur to me to say "Priscilla" or "Allison" or "Julia" or "Ruth" or any of the legions of names more interesting than my own; "Wendy" just pops out of my mouth automatically, as if I didn't even have the wit to enjoy one moment of play-acting, one innocent chance to be someone other than my usual self. (An individual's personality is just a bundle of perceptions held together by habit, Hume argued, but mine seems to be even more habitual than most.) And if I can't be relied upon to produce a meaningless lie, imagine how much less effective I am at producing a lie that would serve a purpose—that would end an argument, say ("Oh, yes, *now* I agree with what you're saying"), or just make someone feel good ("That was a *lovely* poem"). The best I can do under such circumstances is to be silent, and since I have the worst poker face in the world, my silences tend to be all too audible.

I suspect that this lack of inherent kindness is what draws me to kindness in others, not only in David Hume but also in my friend Tom—who, now I come to think of it, bears a resemblance to Hume in other ways as well. He too is given to charitable acts; he too began to write history only after first studying philosophy; he too does not believe in God, and deeply resents the pernicious influence of religion on our daily lives. They even *look* a bit alike, Tom and Hume, or so it seems to me as I examine the famous frontal portrait of David Hume, the one in which he is wearing a white wig and a gold-braided red coat. Tom's face is not as heavy as Hume's—you would never call him portly—but he has the same largeness of countenance, the same thick lower lip, the same calm, light eyes, the same broad, somewhat bumpy forehead, and even, perhaps, the same distinctive nose, neither hooked nor pointed but prominent nonetheless. There is no explaining the physical similarity, for Tom's ancestors are all German Jews, with not a Scot among them. Strangely, Tom is forever mistaking *me* for half-Scottish, and I have to keep reminding him that my red hair is Russian Jewish, and as for my mother's Scottish-sounding name, that came from a second husband who appeared and disappeared during my teens and has never been heard from since. But Tom forgets this every time, perhaps because the one thing he can easily remember about me, the one thing that ties me to his own fact-filled field of endeavor, is that I long ago spent a summer researching Patrick Geddes in the libraries of Edinburgh.

I suppose I was better at facts in those days. It is not that I disbelieve in them now. I am deeply in favor of other people getting their facts right. I resent it when anyone, whether politician or journalist or literary theorist, tries to suggest that the borderline between truth and untruth is irrelevant. However blurred it may be, it is *always* relevant, and the effort to find out exactly where that line is at any given moment is what fuels most of the endeavors I care about. This is the case even with fictional and nonrepresentational artworks: they too need to be true to something. I cannot say exactly how beauty and truth are related, but I know that I believe they are— not in an unchanging way, as Keats seemed to think, but in a way that fluctuates (for me, at any rate) with every year that passes. But to say that truth is changeable does not make it any the less important, or meaningful. Only the pious believe in World Without End; for the rest of us, transitoriness is all we have. This is why Hume's philosophy, which is built up by increments through a series of moment-to-moment observations, is so appropriate to an unbeliever. *Something* is in the details, but it is not God.

I am good at details, by the way; it is just large quantities of undigested facts that get me down. This is why I have trouble reading history (even Hume's charmingly written *History of England* volumes, which I have to put down after a page or two, or my head will begin to feel stuffed), but no trouble at all making a list of everything I need to do for the next day, or week, or month. I run my work-life the way Hume developed his philosophical theories: by imagining myself going through each step in a process, working my way forward along a chain of posited events until I reach a sticking-point, and then working my way back until I find the solution that will free up that stickiness. I did not learn to do this from David Hume, just as I did not learn from my father (or from my best friend, Arthur, who also does it) to add a tip to a restaurant bill that will make the credit-card total come out a round number. We all arrive at our obsessions independently.

Having to get all the details straightened out in advance makes me rather difficult for other people to work with, or even play with. On recreational outings with friends, I am almost always the master planner. I call the box office to buy the necessary tickets well in advance; I calculate backward from the performance time to schedule the departure from home; I make the restaurant reservation at the precise time the show ends, plus ten minutes for transit. On family trips, I generally deal with all travel arrangements, all hotel or apartment accommodations, all dinner plans, all social activities. Occasionally I can cede this kind of responsibility to my friend Arthur (perhaps that is one of the reasons I find it so restful to be with him), but these opportunities to relax my guard do not come often. Mainly, I stay constantly alert to all possible disasters, all potential deviations from the worked-out plan.

My friends and family put up with my managing ways, but as their price for accepting my reign, they insist on poking fun at my excessively linear personality. "I come to you with existential problems, and you offer me hobbies," my old friend Katharine said to me when we were young. She said this in the nicest possible way— that is, truthfully, and affectionately, and with a sardonic acknowledgment that simpleminded practicality or blinkered obtuseness was sometimes just what the situation called for.

My friend Thom Gunn was also a planner of an obsessive sort. It made me feel better that there was someone like him in the world, for Thom was a wild man as well as a planner—a reckless risk-taker with a huge gusto for life, as well as an obsessive detail-monger who carefully kept chaos at bay—and the fact that someone could combine these two sides made me think there might be hope for me yet. Thom wore his wildness on the outside and kept his planning pretty well hidden, so that only those of us who knew him over time could detect just how strong a tendency it was. I remember he once said to me, "I love the idea of being spontaneous, but I just can't manage to do it, so I figure out ways around it, like writing in my pocket diary a week ahead of time, 'Remember to spontaneously ask Mike out to the movies tonight.' "

After Thom died, of causes that may well have stemmed from his own treasured recklessness, Mike asked me and August Kleinzahler, who was one of Thom's closest friends, to go into Thom's study with him and see what was there. We found drawers of file folders containing every draft of every poem he had ever published, all organized chronologically and each clipped to the finished, printed version of the poem; and we found schedules of every reading he had given for the past four decades, each with the list of poems to be read that night typed out neatly in Thom's recognizable typeface. "What a maniac he was," I murmured to August as we looked at this record of obsessiveness, and August nodded, "Yes, he was." It was part of what we both cherished about him, but it was rarely visible in such a naked form.

Since Thom died, I have often thought about him in connection with David Hume. It is not that they were superficially alike. Despite Thom's Scottish name (it was really Thomson Gunn), he did not look anything like Hume, though perhaps he looked the way the very young Hume had, lean and tall and rawboned. Nor would anyone have classified Thom as a philosopher: he didn't like to think abstractly, but saw everything in its particulars, whether it had happened to him yesterday or to someone else four hundred years ago. Thom's was a world of sensory experience—experience that could be converted, in his wonderful poems, into language, but that had not been undergone for the sake of language. The felt experience was the primary thing, for Thom. So you can see that if he were to resemble *any* philosopher, it would have been David Hume.

But what made me associate him with Hume was something else: his goodness. Like Hume, Thom was not boringly, cloyingly good. He had a sharp tongue and a cold eye, and he could use them to scathing effect. He also adored misbehavior, and tried to practice it himself, though often his innate courtesy and his sense of decorum held him back. He would have liked to be worse than he was, and I'm not sure he would have liked being called good. But that's what he was.

As with Hume, this goodness came out partly in the

form of well-concealed generosity. For most of his life, Thom had very little money, but when he finally came into some (he won a five-year MacArthur Award in his sixties), he began to give it away like mad. He even gave some of it to me, or rather, to *The Threepenny Review*, which he supported at a far higher level than he could afford. And he began sending monthly checks to a brilliant, erratic poet of our acquaintance, a man who was often, or always, out of work, because he felt that the poet needed money and he, Thom, had it to give. He told me about the monthly checks in confidence, and said he didn't want anyone else to know about them, but now that he is dead I feel I can expose his generosity. When I first learned that he had died—quite suddenly, in the night—I wondered about all the other secrets he had taken with him.

Because Thom was so good, people loved him wholeheartedly, even though we knew him only partially, at best. He put more of himself into his poems than he did into his daily conversation, or rather, he put into them a side of himself, the self-knowing, self-analytic, painfully aware side, that he did not care to show to the people around him. Did not care to, or couldn't: I'm not sure which. This habit of enclosure made him seem a bit removed from things, a bit inaccessible, even when he was at his warmest and jolliest. (He had a huge laugh; I can hear it still, if I try.) He was a very important friend to me, but I'm not sure I would have called the friendship intimate. I think he loved me, though, and I know I loved him.

One of the things he always used to say, a sort of commentary on the nature of our friendship, was that we had both been brought up as agnostics. It was as if this made us special, and different: we had never had a shred of religious belief, but had come by our atheism naturally and originally, without having to react against piety and discover disbelief by default. Something about our shared irreligion, and something about the way he died (probably of a heart attack, probably after taking drugs—not suicide, but a choice of a different kind; endlessly searching for pleasure, disregarding the effects of speed on a seventy-four-year-old heart, not particularly wishing to grow old ungracefully; alive in his garden rereading *A Sentimental Education* one day, and gone, completely gone, the next), and something about the wholehearted quality of my feelings for him, which were not fraught and complicated like my feelings for most people, but gentle and consistent and undivided—all this has made his death, for me, somehow simpler to take in. I was shocked when I heard about it, and I was very sad for many months after, and I still feel sad whenever I hear or see or read something I would have liked to tell him about. But I very soon came to the realization that though his death was a bad thing for those of us he had left behind, it was not a bad thing for him. He was simply non-existent: not at peace, not with God, not enjoying eternal rest, not haunting his former life. Nothing. I began to understand, for the first time, what Hume had meant about Lucretius.

I find it strange that people associate morality with religion. By "morality" I don't mean moralizing, or moral self-righteousness. I mean the desire to do good in the world, to be as fair and generous as possible, even to make a few self-sacrifices if they are not excruciatingly painful and can actually be of some use. Most of the people who have this kind of morality, in my experience, also have a pretty solid respect for the pleasures of existence, their own and others'. They are not ascetics or saints: their generosity and goodness stem from an overflow of sympathy and good spirits, a feeling that other people deserve to enjoy the things they themselves enjoy. And most of the people whom I would call moral in this way are not at all religious.

Just think about it logically for a moment. Is it admirable to be benevolent toward others because you hope for a payback in the afterlife—or, conversely, to refrain from unpleasant behavior because you're afraid of eternal damnation? Greed and fear do not seem to me to be good supports on which to build a system of ethical behavior, yet the carrot and the stick are clearly at the core of most religious instruction. I am sure there *are* morally admirable people who believe in God, but I would argue that the two qualities are entirely separable, and probably separate, in most characters; the link is at best coincidental and at worst inverse. We can all think of badly behaved people who believed in God, starting with the Inquisition and ending with yesterday's news. Yet vast numbers of my fellow citizens continue to think that going to church will make them—or me—into a better person. I even have acquaintances who had pretty much given up on religion themselves but then went *back* to church after their children were born, ostensibly so that the children would have some kind of moral framework in their lives. Why didn't these people understand that a sense of moral responsibility could emerge from day-to-day relations between human beings, without any necessity for a supervising, admonitory, favorites-playing God?

Monotheism has always struck me as a step in the wrong direction, in that, unlike polytheism, it posits an all-knowing God who can't be wrong. Such a person would have a lot to answer for in the evil-that-gets-done-in-the-world department, and simply inventing a devil to address that side of the problem only exacerbates it. Christianity, in this sense, is even more illogical than Judaism. But I don't want to get involved in denominational quibbling. Any church or synagogue or mosque, any fount of worship devoted to a singular all-powerful God, gives me the heebie-jeebies. Yet I don't feel at all this way about the old Greek temples I've visited, the ones at Paestum, Segesta, Agrigento, and Olympia (though I'm not sure that's because their gods are less objectionable to begin with: they might just be less objectionable because they're dead).

The other night, as I sat watching a very good performance of *Die Walküre,* it dawned on me how brilliant of Wagner it was to set his grand myth among ancient, multiple gods. His Wotan is a willful, demanding, oppressively authoritarian figure—in this respect, not unlike Yahweh or Milton's God. But he is also torn by emotion, wrenched by conflicting obligations, doomed by his own passions, and betrayed by his own sworn oaths, and that makes him a far more interesting figure than either of those two solitary Gods. If Wotan were colder and more consistent, he might be a better god and a better ruler of the gods, but he would be much less appealing to us, the mortals out in the audience.

The two tragedies at the heart of *Die Walküre*—first the death of Siegmund, Wotan's half-mortal son, and then Wotan's renunciation of his favorite child, Brünnhilde—are both set in motion by the intervention of another god: that is, Fricka, Wotan's legal wife. Like Juno in the classical myths (and, even more, like Junon in the French neoclassical versions), Fricka is the embodiment of jealousy; but unlike Juno's, her jealousy has a steely, lawyerlike logic to support it. With serpentile cleverness, she uses Wotan's own arguments and assertions against him, making him feel that if he helps Siegmund survive, he will undermine his own power by contradicting his stated principles. She also, cunningly, gets him to order Brünnhilde not to give Siegmund any aid either, because she knows that Wotan's Valkyrie daughter (who is, quite pointedly, not *her* daughter) reflects everything strong and good about him, including his love for Siegmund. Fricka plays on her husband's desire to believe that even Brünnhilde, his most wonderful creation, is merely an extension of his own will—and when Brünnhilde violates that belief by standing up for Siegmund, he strips her of her immortality and cuts her off for good.

The bare-bones plot is implausible at best (I have left out the whole incestuous love affair between Siegmund and his sister Sieglinde, though that too is central to the plot, and to the implausibility), and without the music it would be merely ridiculous. But the music makes us able to feel Wotan's despair as if it were Lear's, even as we are also feeling Siegmund's and Brünnhilde's—for that is part of what it means for a tragedy to be Shakespearean. And it is because Wotan is one god among many, rather than a single all-powerful god, that he can become this kind of psychologically realized character. It would be too simplistic to say that his flaws make him human; rather, let us say that as he sacrifices his beloved child by making her mortal, he feels the pain of that sacrifice in a way that we can't quite imagine God-the-father feeling about Christ. The difference is that Wotan, despite his stature as an immortal, is not in control of events: he is caught in the toils of his own character, his own inconsistent desire for consistency, so that he is finally just as much a victim of fate and coincidence as his less powerful children are.

> We are placed in this world, as in a great theatre, where the true springs and causes of every event are entirely concealed from us; nor have we either sufficient wisdom

to foresee, or power to prevent these ills, with which we are continually threatened. We hang in perpetual suspense between life and death, health and sickness, plenty and want; which are distributed amongst the human species by secret and unknown causes, whose operation is oft unexpected, and always unaccountable. These *unknown causes,* then, become the constant object of our hope and fear; and while the passions are kept in perpetual alarm by an anxious expectation of events, the imagination is equally employed in forming ideas of those powers, on which we have so entire a dependence.

This paragraph of acute Wagnerian criticism is in fact a passage from David Hume's essay "The Natural History of Religion"—specifically, a paragraph drawn from the section on the origins of polytheism. I came to this essay, as you might guess, expecting to get to the heart of my feeling for Hume. Here at last, I imagined, would be the firm arguments of the rational agnostic I saw as my ally; here is where I would find the reigning eighteenth-century Christianity shoved bravely aside.

What I found was something much stranger and less reassuring. Indeed, it would not be an exaggeration to say that the niggling suspicion that I was *not* going to write a book about David Hume first came upon me when I read (or re-read, because I had owned it for thirty years) this essay. "The Natural History of Religion" argues, first of all, that the progress of mankind "from rude beginnings to a state of greater perfection" involves a corresponding move from polytheistic to monotheistic religion. The essay even contains within its first few pages a sentence that goes: "It seems certain, that, according to the natural progress of human thought, the ignorant multitude must first entertain some grovelling and familiar notion of superior powers, before they stretch their conception to that perfect Being, who bestowed order on the whole frame of nature."

I was appalled. Aside from its shameless pandering to the audience, its apparent support of the contemporary belief in a capitalized, singular Supreme Being, the sentence was irksomely snobbish in its attitude toward the grovelling multitude. I had actually seen this snobbery of Hume's before, in some of the personal letters—letters about his own family's standing in Scotland, say, or about someone else's good breeding or lack thereof—but I had mentally ditched the evidence as irrelevant to his philosophy. Now, however, I was confronted with that very tone *in* the philosophy, and in an argument that favored monotheism to boot.

But did it really favor monotheism? As I read along, it became harder and harder to tell. A wickedly ironic sense of humor seemed to lap at the edges of every argument, like a fire that threatened to consume the whole enterprise. About midway through the essay, Hume tossed off the comment:

> It must be allowed, that the ROMAN CATHOLICS are a very learned sect; and that no one communion, but that of the Church of ENGLAND, can dispute their being the most learned of all the Christian churches: Yet AVERROËS, the famous ARABIAN, who, no doubt, had heard of the EGYPTIAN superstition, declares, that of all religions, the most absurd and nonsensical is that, whose votaries eat, after having created, their deity.

The word "communion" is doing very heavy duty in this passage—and in the guise of questioning Catholic practice, Hume manages to get at *all* the Christian churches, in part by allowing a non-Christian to deliver the devastating critique. (Averroës, though not necessarily famous to us, is an altogether serious source: a twelfth-century Spanish Moor, he was a classical scholar as well as a respected judge.) But how does this interjection in any way support the idea that monotheism represents progress? It patently doesn't. The so-called argument of the essay has swallowed its own tail, leaving the author nowhere to go but into a kind of stand-up comedy routine in which he proceeds to tell catechism jokes with punchlines like: *"How many Gods are there?" "None at all! . . . You have told me all along that there is but one God: And yesterday I eat him."*

I did not know how to take any of this. Was this the way to make a philosophical argument against religion? Was this the kind of help I had been hoping to get from Hume My Contemporary? God forbid. And yet even as I collapsed in dismay, I also realized that Hume had once again evaded expectations. He was not to be pinned down to any system of thought, even mine; he was not going to allow himself to be merely useful. The Hume I had in mind when I started thinking about the book was a relatively straightforward fellow—I had vaguely imagined I would find a rational explicator who built up his arguments in logical steps—whereas, instead, I was faced with a stylish littérateur who allowed his essay to be pulled hither and yon as each new idea struck him. I had set out looking for Locke's smarter cousin, but I had ended up with the twin brother of Montaigne.

My admiration for Montaigne is unmitigated, but it tends to be expressed in acts of omission rather than commission. I do not, that is, often find myself reading

Montaigne, though whenever I do read him, I can see that he's beyond compare. Perhaps it's those scrupulous, fact-brandishing footnotes of his that scare me off; or perhaps it's my sense that by reading him in English— the only way I could possibly read him—I am missing everything that truly matters in his style. That can't be true, though, because he always seems to be recogniz- ably Montaigne (just as Proust is always recognizably Proust) no matter whose translation I read. So some- thing must be getting through.

When I first discerned the secret connection between Hume and Montaigne, I thought it could be my way in. I picked up the huge Screech edition of Montaigne and settled in for a nice long read, starting with the famous "Apology for Raymond Sebond." Soon I put it down again. I just wasn't up to a hundred and ninety-five pages of this undulating thought process. On the shorter essays, maybe, I could manage to stick with Montaigne as he raced around three or four or even five violent switchbacks, but over the longer haul I began to feel car- sick. I admit that this was my fault and not Montaigne's. My linear brain just wasn't up to his flexible sinuosity. But such admissions accomplish nothing: I still couldn't manage to read him straight through. My admiration for Montaigne, it seemed, would have to remain largely theoretical, and so would any insights I might have about the connection between his style and Hume's.

Who, in any case, would have cared about my discovery? It wouldn't matter to the philosophers, since I am not one of them; and it certainly wouldn't matter to anyone else. Perhaps, if my old friend Lenny were still alive, it would have mattered to him, but I'm not even sure of that—he had his Montaigne, and I had my Hume, and we were both too old (or would have been, if he were still alive) to start mixing and matching. Realizing this made me feel briefly lonely, but the loneliness was not, in fact, another symptom of missing Lenny. It was a much more narcissistic feeling than that. I missed the possibility of a more flexible self.

It's odd that Hume had brought me to this, because when I began thinking of him, it was precisely as a defender of one of my rigidly held beliefs (atheism being as much of a conviction as any other). I thought that by writing about him I would somehow prove the case for religious doubt, or at least be closer to arriving at a proof. But that kind of lockbox logic—the kind, in effect, in which most professional philosophy has now enclosed itself—is exactly what Hume turned out to be an escape from. If he had anything to teach me at all, it was about the value of *not* arriving at a firm conclusion.

I hesitate even to use words like "teach" and "value" in this context, for fear of seeming to ally myself with some cockamamie School of Practical Philosophy. There is, as it happens, a real organization of that name. It advertises itself, mainly in placards on the New York subway, as a place that

> takes the master philosophies of East and West and examines how they can be put to immediate use. It draws on the great teachers of mankind who have always taught about the true nature of man, his purpose in the world, and how to live a happy, content and useful life. Above all, it is PRACTICAL Philosophy, and so it is easy to test in experience and to apply in daily life.

Riding the subway one recent October and reading this dreck, I began to have serious doubts about my Hume project. Was *this* what I had thought of doing with him—putting him to immediate use, applying him in daily life? No wonder he had resisted me. And no wonder the professional philosophers had retreated to the level of *if p then not not-p,* with these promises and slogans ("It is *philosophy* that guides and inspires the finest life") as their perceived alternative. It began to seem a kind of paradox: I could only be taught something by

David Hume if I tried very hard not to think about him as having something to teach.

But why need this be such a difficult prospect? I am used to thinking of novels, movies, plays, and operas in this way. The more their moral tone is evident, the less I trust them. I want to sink myself into their element, be unwittingly influenced by them, and feel at least two different, contradictory effects by the time I emerge. I do not expect, in that sense, to be taught by works of art, except insofar as that verb can be broadly applied to *any* kind of mental transformation.

I have not always felt this way. When I was very young and took the nineteenth-century novelists as my only standard, I often demanded to know what the moral of something was. But increasingly, as I grow older, I find myself less insistent on comprehensible moral instruction and more drawn to things I can't fully understand. An unfortunate side-effect of this recent preference for indirection is that I'm becoming a worse and worse classroom instructor. That is, on those relatively few occasions when I am called upon to teach, I seem less and less able to do it. Faced with remarkable works of literature, I find I can no longer explicate them: I just want to set them out and have them taken up as their own Exhibit A, their own best defense. (The other day, hiding in the ladies' room during one of the seemingly endless sessions of a seminar I was guest-professoring, I overheard two of my students chatting about me in the adjoining cubicles. "She's obviously very intelligent," said one, "but all she ever says is that things are 'interesting.'" The remark cut me to the quick, in part because it seemed so accurate.)

I don't know why I should have expected David Hume's writing to be any more instructive or useful than other works of art. What drew me to him in the first place, after all, was that he thought of himself as a literary man as well as a philosopher. Or rather, he was a philosopher *because* he was a literary man, and vice versa. The two impulses, in him, did not come apart. In his brief autobiographical "My Own Life," written just before he died, Hume mentions that he "was seized very early with a passion for literature, which has been the ruling passion of my life, and the great source of my enjoyments." Then, in the very next sentence, he reintroduces this passion as "an unsurmountable aversion to everything but the pursuits of philosophy and general learning"—as if these two pursuits *were* literature, or its direct translation.

Some of the seeming contradiction, of course, stems from a change in vocabulary: what Hume meant by "literature" might more commonly be called either "writing" or "scholarship" today. But those two modern substitutes are themselves far from identical, and even the shift from a single term to two masks a whole set of attitudes about professional experts, their readers, and the function of literary style. We live, now, on the other side of that divide, but Hume's imagined readership had not yet split apart into people who studied philosophy because it was their job to do so, and people who read essays because they wanted to hear a voice speaking to them. In his mind (or perhaps it was only in his wishful longings), these audiences were still one.

That the rot had begun to set in even in Hume's lifetime is suggested by his own essay called "Of Essay Writing." In this odd little piece—one of the things he pointedly left out of his collected writings, though it had appeared briefly in an 1742 edition of his *Essays Moral, Political, and Literary*—he complained about the divison between lively society and the world of scholarship. Or, as he said:

The Separation of the Learned from the conversible World seems to have been the great Defect of the last Age, and must have had a very bad Influence both on Books and Company: For what Possibility is there of finding Topics of Conversation fit for the Entertainment of rational Creatures, without having Recourse sometimes to History, Poetry, Politics, and the more obvious Principles, at least, of Philosophy? . . . On the other Hand, Learning has been as great a Loser by being shut up in Colleges and Cells, and secluded from the World and good Company. By that means, every thing of what we call *Belles Lettres* became totally barbarous, being cultivated by Men without any Taste of Life or Manners, and without that Liberty and Facility of Thought and Expression, which can only be acquir'd by Conversation.

A valid complaint even now—though there is a slight taint of Humean snobbery in that allusion to Manners. But leaving aside the class issues (always hard to do with Hume, which may be in part why I abandoned him), leaving aside the question of *whose* richly laden dinner tables and well-appointed salons are to provide the ideal forums for Conversation, I would still want to insist that he has a point here. We too are starved for intelligent conversation—which Hume identifies, in this essay, with *female* conversation. (He obviously means this as a compliment, but the compliment feels ever-so-slightly patronizing, and I like to think that it could even have been his eventual awareness of this bad-faith tone which made him decide to withdraw the essay—though in saying this

I'm probably just reading my own biases into his, as I am so often tempted to do.) And that kind of conversation, that kind of intelligence, can't arise if the scholars and the society ladies, the professionals and the amateurs, the people who look deeply into one small thing and the people who skate gracefully over many, do not pool their resources.

The fact that Hume could write this essay at all suggests that he thought the situation could still be retrieved. Or maybe he thought so, and then thought better. Perhaps *this*, finally, is why he chose to suppress "Of Essay Writing": because the essay itself seems to attribute so much power to its own form, in a manner that is both immodest and inaccurate. The salvation of the culture, the joining of the "learned" and the "conversible," cannot reasonably be said to rest in the hands of the essayist.

And if such writing could not, in the end, alleviate the problem in Hume's time, it certainly cannot in ours. The gap has widened even further now; the degree of slippage has only increased. You can see this, for instance, in Hume's casual assumptions about "what we call *Belles Lettres.*" It's clear from the way he words the passage that history, poetry, politics, and philosophy—the things he is classifying as belles lettres—also qualify as learned scholarship. That the two could be considered equivalent would deeply surprise twenty-first-century academics, who tend to use *belles-lettristic* as one of their chief terms of abuse, a rough synonym for *not serious* or *suspiciously well-written*.

If I sound excessively grumpy about this, it's because I am. I know it shouldn't matter to me what academics do, since I am not one of them. It certainly doesn't matter to most of America, or even to most of the English-speaking world. But the things I care about are so closely allied to the pursuits of academia that I find it painful to acknowledge the vast degree of separation between us. Like Hume, I long for a world in which the things I am interested in and the things people study in universities could be considered overlapping, if not identical—whereas they only seem to be getting farther and farther apart, so that from my present vantage point Hume's period looks like a golden age, even if he found it less than satisfactory.

Part of what I long for is that "interestingness" (for the student was right, this quality is key for me) should be something that matters. To be interesting is to be interesting *to* someone, to have a relationship with one's audience. I am not saying I manage to practice this consistently myself, but it is still a standard I apply to the artworks and experiences I care about. It is a standard that cannot be standardized, because it all comes down to what the individual reader or listener or watcher finds interesting. And yet it is crucial all the same. This is what I constantly find myself trying to explain to academics, generally with no success. They always seem to be trying to get rid of what they call the "personal element" in forming judgments, whereas I am always trying to put it back in.

I have lived, for most of my adult life, in the ever-widening no-man's-land between the kingdom of Learning and the realm of Conversation. It is more than likely that the desire to bridge the gap between these two worlds had a large part in making me want to write a book about David Hume, and it is equally likely that the impossibility of building such a bridge is what prevented me, in the end, from writing it.

I have a Scottish friend named James—Jim, he's called, by everyone who knows him. He has not lived in Scotland for many years, but he still thinks of himself as deeply Scottish (even unconsciously, if thought can be said to be unconscious). In the weekly column he writes for a London periodical, he almost always inserts an anecdote about a Scottish writer or a piece of Scottish news or an event in Scottish history, and I always wonder, when I read these mentions, whether he is doing it on purpose, or whether the decision to include such items just comes over him afresh each week, as if for the first time. Though he now lives some distance from his native Glasgow, Jim faithfully celebrates Burns Day every January; I believe he's even taught his Russian wife to cook haggis. When he drinks heavily into the night (as he did the night he learned of Thom Gunn's death, for he loved Thom Gunn), his favorite tipple is a good malt Scotch. And he still *sounds* Scottish, even after more than half a lifetime spent in England and France.

When I told Jim that I was thinking of writing a book about David Hume, he seemed pleased if skeptical. (The Scots are always skeptical, even about the things that give them the most pleasure—perhaps especially about those things.) And then, when I told him why I was giving it up, he was scathing in the best Scottish manner: "He turned out to be 'too stuck in the eighteenth century' for you? My god, what did you expect?" (I am not going to reproduce the Scottish pronunciation—I detest dialogue that is written in dialect—but you can imagine it for yourself.) "Did you think David Hume was going to be a contemporary San Franciscan, all warm and cozy and politically correct? Are you shocked at his old-fashioned opinions? Is that what you mean by calling him 'snob-bish'?" And so on, in that vein.

I was both miffed and amused by this tirade, both embarrassed and defensive. What *had* I thought? What had I actually wanted Hume to do for me? Was it, in fact, wrong of me to have wanted anything at all from him? Was practicality inimical to scholarship?

I still don't know the answer to this. It would be sim-plest to answer that final question with a yes, to say that biographical and critical investigation needs to be disin-terested if it is to be any good at all. But it is not in me to yield on this point entirely. Something about the nature of my own enterprise in life—the way I find myself imposing my personality on everything around me and observing things through the screen of that personality—makes me believe in the ineradicability of the individual perspective. And Hume, in a grand and disinterested way, has encouraged me in that belief.

So let me go back to the earlier question and ask again, seriously, what it was I thought Hume could do for me. Prove me right? But he was not in the business of proving anything. Offer me underlying principles of judgment? Nix on that one, too. Give me access to a lost world in which the life of the mind and the life of art and the life of sensory pleasure still seemed to be connected?

Ah. So that was it. It was not Hume who had failed to be sufficiently modern, but I who could not reach backward in time to clasp that eighteenth-century hand. I was stuck here, now, in this place with all its shortcomings, in this time with all its flaws.

Sometimes, when I have felt particularly despairing about the present moment, I have cheered myself up with the thought that we do, after all, still have all the great artworks that came before us. We can read Henry James and David Hume, we can go to an Ibsen play or a Handel opera, and they are as alive for us, as present *to* us, as they could ever be to anyone. This is one of the terrific things about art: it takes you out of yourself, and for the duration of your encounter with it (if it is a successful encounter), you are transformed into something or someone slightly outside of time. It lets you feel there are occasional escape hatches from the tunnel-like plod to the grave, unexpected side-exits off the otherwise one-way street.

There is something pathetic, though, about someone whose best friends, at the present moment in time, are Henry James and David Hume. I want to have living friends, too. I want the conversation to be mutual and permeable to change. I want to feel that other people, alive right now, care about the same things I do. This, perhaps, is why I keep returning to the performing arts, seeking out the kind of experience you can only get at plays and operas and concerts—the sense that there is a living bond connecting the people in the audience and the people onstage, making them all a party to an event which is also a feeling and at the same time a critical response. Attending a performance can, at its best, annihilate the gap I've been complaining about: between the eighteenth century and now, between learning and conversation, between thought and feeling, between the living and the dead.

Not that this happens every time. In fact, it almost never happens. (I am reminded of the moment in *Through the Looking Glass* where Alice and the Gnat are talking about the Bread-and-butter-fly, which lives on weak tea with cream and will die if it can't find any. "'But that must happen very often,' Alice remarked thoughtfully. 'It always happens,' said the Gnat.") But when it does happen, the feeling of lift-off—of being taken out of yourself, transported to a new plane of existence, filled with exhilaration and energy and delight—is practically unduplicatable. Hume has an essay called "Of Tragedy" wherein he ponders the old question about why we like to watch tragic events onstage when we don't at all enjoy witnessing them in real life. His answer, to the extent he finds one, has something to do with the fact that tragedy is an imitation, and "imitation is always itself agreeable." I am not sure that I believe this. But I do agree with something else Hume says: that the exercise of human ingenuity, in piecing together a performed tragedy at its highest level, is itself pleasurable for other humans to watch. Or, as Hume puts it,

> the genius required to paint objects in a lively manner, the art employed in collecting all the pathetic circumstances, the judgment displayed in disposing them: the exercise, I say, of all these noble talents, together with the force of expression, and the beauty of oratorical numbers, diffuse the highest satisfaction on the audience . . . By this means, the uneasiness of the melancholy passions is not only overpowered and effaced by something stronger of an opposite kind; but the whole impulse of those passions is converted into pleasure, and swells the delight which the eloquence raises in us.

As with most excellent criticism, there is no way of proving this assertion right or wrong, but at the very least it is psychologically astute. I have no doubt that something like this plays a part in my own strongly felt responses to the best performances I've seen, and I think it holds true for movies and books as well as plays. The sense of being placed in authoritative hands—led through the tragic experience by an intelligent and sensitive guide—cushions us from the most painful kind of grief even as it allows us to submit ourselves to another, softer, more enjoyable kind of sadness. So the connection one feels in such cases is not just with the other members of an actual audience, but also with the maker of the art-work, and through him with all the other potential audience members on whom the work will have a similar effect.

The situation is more complicated with music. Though music can obviously make you feel sad, it is not clear that it can be tragic in Hume's sense of the word. This is not only because there is no way of knowing what an eloquent "imitation" would mean in such a context (what, exactly, could music be imitating, when it seems so clearly to *be* the thing itself?), but also because the springs of our reaction to music lie deeper than thought. I sometimes think that I have felt more, listening to some pieces of music, than I have at any other kind of performance—and I am not, as I have said, a particularly musical person. Part of what music allows me is the freedom to drift off into a reverie of my own, stimulated but not constrained by the inventions of the composer. And part of what I love about music is the way it relaxes the usual need to understand. Sometimes the pleasure of an artwork comes from *not* knowing, *not* understanding, *not* recognizing.

There is something I have not told you yet about that performance of the Brahms Requiem, the one I heard in Berlin the first time I visited the Philharmoniker hall. I have said that it had a powerful effect on me, but what I didn't tell you—what I didn't, perhaps, recognize myself until just this minute—was that the core of this whole book lay in that prolonged moment of listening. I went to Berlin thinking that I would write about David Hume there (as I always, for the past few years, have gone everywhere thinking I would write about David Hume). But as I sat in that acoustically perfect auditorium, feeling the waves of music pour over me—listening with my whole body, it seemed, and not just with my ears—I realized that I was going to have to write about Lenny instead.

I had been carrying around Lenny's death in a locked package up till then, a locked, frozen package that I couldn't get at but couldn't throw away, either. As long as I was afraid to look inside the package, it maintained its terrifying hold over me: it frightened and depressed me, or would have done, if I had allowed myself to have even *those* feelings instead of their shadowy half-versions. It wasn't just Lenny that had been frozen; I had, too. But as

I sat in the Berlin Philharmonic hall and listened to the choral voices singing their incomprehensible words, something warmed and softened in me. I became, for the first time in months, able to feel strongly again.

Later, when I looked at the words in the program, I saw that the choral voices had been singing about the triumph of God over death. This is what I mean about the importance of not understanding. If I had known this at the time, I might have stiffened my atheist spine and resisted. But instead of taking in what the German words meant, I just allowed them to echo through my body: I *felt* them, quite literally, instead of understanding them. And the reverie I fell into as I listened to Brahms's music was not about God triumphing over death, but about music and death grappling with each other. Death was chasing me, and I was fleeing from it, and it was pounding toward me; it was pounding *in* the music, but the music was also what was helping me to flee. And, as in a myth or a fairy tale, I sensed that what would enable me to escape—not forever, because all such escapes are temporary, but to escape just this once—would be if I looked death, Lenny's death, in the face: if I turned back and looked at it as clearly and sustainedly as I could bear.

But then it seemed that this was not enough. I could

not just settle with Lenny—or rather, in order to settle with him, I had to work my way back through that transitional moment, through Berlin and through David Hume. And then, having let go of all three of them (there are always three, in fairy tales), I could rest.

Part Three

DIFFICULT
FRIENDS

"His love of Ravelstein had a dark side. It would not be love otherwise. . . ."

—"On Ravelstein"

I have never watched anyone else die. I am not going to say much about the details of Lenny's dying, mainly because I promised not to. Or at least I made some kind of promise to him, and I am keeping it in my own way.

One afternoon, when he was still quite coherent and I still believed he might survive, I sat with him for a few hours in the hospital. (His wife, who had been maintaining a round-the-clock vigil, had finally given in to our collective pleas and allowed some of us to substitute while she rested.) Occasionally Lenny and I would exchange a few words of conversation, and occasionally I would do some small thing for him at his request, but mostly he just lay there while I read.

I remember that I had just turned the page when I heard Lenny say something. I got up from my chair and approached his bed (I had been sitting at a distance so as not to breathe germs on him), and I asked him to repeat what he had said. In the hoarse whisper that was all that now remained of his memorable voice, he said something that I took to be "Nobody ever writes about this."

"Nobody ever writes about this?" I parroted back.

"You—you." In his effort to make it emphatic, the word came out as "Jew," but I knew what he meant. "You. Never write about this."

I was momentarily shocked by Lenny's statement, but there was also something strangely familiar about it, and later that day, after I got home from the hospital, I realized why. In *Patrimony,* Philip Roth's book about his father's life and death, he tells us that his father made him promise not to write about a particularly grotesque incident that took place during his final illness. Philip Roth breaks the promise—he gives us, in *Patrimony,* every embarrassing detail—and part of how you feel about this book of Roth's is bound to be influenced by how you feel about this violation. I am sure Lenny hated that aspect of the book, but I am equally sure he was not alluding to that passage when he made his statement to me, since it was not a moment that called for or even tolerated literary allusion.

When Lenny said this to me, I responded by saying that of course I would never write about it. Trying to be encouraging, I said that it was *his* experience to write about if he wished, or not—that my only reason for being there was as his friend, and that I wasn't there as a writer or editor or any of the other roles he had known me in. Still, I knew, even as I said this, that Lenny would not write about it. "Death is not a subject," he kept saying, with a kind of depressed, surprised horror, in the days after he first heard the diagnosis. And in his own terms, he was right. Much as he had loved and trusted the written word, it had nothing now to offer him.

Even to describe what Lenny asked of me is, I realize, to open myself up to the charge of betrayal. But silence, which became Lenny's only alternative, does not now seem to me adequate. His death has been so important to me, in ways I am just beginning to work out, that I can't simply let it go. So I have chosen to take my promise as applying to the particulars of dying: those horrible, shameful, personal details that anyone who has spent time in a hospital knows about. These you will not hear from me. But that he died is a fact in my life, still, now.

I would not have expected Lenny's death to affect me so strongly. This sounds colder than it is meant to. It is not that I was not extremely fond of him. I would even say I loved him, in the way one loves people whom one takes for granted and doesn't necessarily see often. Though he was not actually related to me, the bond felt familial. He was funny and smart in familiar ways, and he was annoying in familiar ways. He was like the old uncle, growing deaf and indulging in a bit too much wine, who picks fights with everyone else at the Passover dinner table. (I do not know my own uncles, and I rarely attend a seder, but this is how I imagine such a family life to be.) You could tell Lenny that he was full of shit, and he would laugh. I thought he would be around forever.

In this, perhaps, I was borrowing his own views. Lenny was a bit of a hypochondriac, and he often talked and wrote and thought about death, but at the core of his being he did not really believe he would ever die. He was not religious—and by this I mean that, though he very much identified himself as a Jew, he did not practice any of the rituals of Judaism, or of any other religion, for that matter. But he was intensely superstitious: he thought that evil or vicious actions brought on punishments, and he considered death the most extreme of these punishments. "See!" he would say when a critic who had reviewed him badly died an agonizing and premature death. "That's what happens to all my enemies." This was only partly a joke. And since dying was a punishment meted out for bad behavior, Lenny had no sense (except for his literary, intellectual, philosophical sense, which was profound) of the inevitability of death.

When he lay unconscious in the hospital, technically still alive but clearly only a few hours or days away from death, I had a conversation with his daughter, Louisa, about the funeral. Lenny's mother—who, at ninety, was still very much alive—wanted a Jewish funeral, a burial in the ground within three days of the death. Lenny's half-Jewish children and non-Jewish wife would have preferred cremation, but they hesitated to push their views too hard.

"I just wish I knew what my dad would have wanted," Louisa said to me. "I wish he would wake up for a minute so I could ask him whether he'd rather be buried or cremated." In her half-joking, half-serious suggestion, I heard a strong echo of her father.

"Oh, Louisa," I said. "You know if you had ever asked him that, he would just have rolled his eyes in that way he had. He would never have chosen, because he always thought there was some other option—some way out other than dying."

I suppose intense fear of death and disbelief in one's own death are two sides of the same coin. The discovery that he himself was dying was an unbearable shock for Lenny. It did not fit in with any reasonable system of rewards and punishments, even Lenny's system, in which the rewards were small and infrequent, the punishments huge and relentless (Lenny's God, if he existed, was definitely a jealous god).

Certain rare people seem able to face their own deaths with equanimity. One of these, apparently, was David Hume, who wrote in his little essay "My Own Life," shortly before his own death:

> In spring 1775, I was struck with a Disorder in my Bowels, which at first gave me no Alarm, but has since, as I apprehend it, become mortal and incurable. I now reckon upon a speedy Dissolution. I have suffered very little pain from my Disorder; and what is more strange, have, notwithstanding the great Decline of my Person, never suffered a Moments Abatement of my Spirits: Insomuch, that were I to name the Period of my Life which I should most choose to pass over again I might be tempted to point to this later Period. I possess the same Ardor as ever in Study, and the same Gaiety in Company. I consider besides, that a Man of sixty five, by dying, cuts off only a few Years of Infirmities: And though I see many symptoms of my literary Reputation's breaking out at last with additional Lustre, I know, that I had but few Years to enjoy it. It is difficult to be more detached from Life than I am at present.
>
> To conclude historically with my own Character—I am, or rather was (for that is the Style, I must now use in speaking of myself; which emboldens me the more to

speak my Sentiments) I was, I say, a man of mild Dispositions, of Command of Temper, of an open, social, and cheerful Humour, capable of Attachment, but little susceptible of Enmity, and of great Moderation in all my Passions.

Nothing could sound less like Lenny. And now, reading over that Hume quotation once again, I realize something else about it: nothing could sound less like me. For I too, like Lenny, am a difficult friend. I too have little Command of Temper and no Moderation in my Passions. Perhaps that is why his dying has so possessed me.

Certainly it explains why we quarreled so many times. And when I say quarreled, I do not mean a brief spat. Each of our quarrels was epic in length, lasting a minimum of a year and in some cases four or five years. During these periods we would not speak to each other at all. And then, when we began speaking again, we resumed the friendship as if it had never been interrupted. We disregarded those wordless years casually, easily, as if we had all the time in the world. Each of us perhaps imagined that we did.

2.

"Personally, I'm more interested in the past than in visions of the future, which is, I'm afraid, ultimately the same for all of us."

—*Time Out of Mind*

I can no longer remember the exact timing of the quarrels, but I am pretty sure that the first one involved the movie of *The Men's Club*. Lenny published a number of books in his lifetime, but he only published one novel, and that was by far his worst book. It had redeeming features—when he read aloud from it, you could fall out of your seat laughing at the hilarious bits—but overall it was not a success in any way except financially. Compared to the movie that was made from it, however, it was a great work of art. I am not sure I've ever seen a worse movie than *The Men's Club*. Even now, watching Stockard Channing as the First Lady on *The West Wing*, I feel a slight revulsion which can be traced back, I suspect, to her role in that terrible movie. And the other actors, some of them very good actors, were equally hopeless in the face of the intractable material.

My quarrel with Lenny started before the movie was ever made. Perhaps I should back up and say that we became friends after I was his student, first in a graduate research methods class and then in a creative writing seminar. Lenny was not, strictly speaking, a good teacher— I learned nothing about research methods from him, and very little about creative writing—but he had a way of reading aloud a line of Wallace Stevens, say, or Kafka, that would change forever your understanding of a poem or story. His voice was his greatest pedagogical instrument. On the other hand, he excused every class early, without exception. I don't think I ever saw him last to the end of the hour.

But if I am really to arrive at the origins of our friendship, I must go back even further, to the summer of 1975, when I was about to start graduate school at Berkeley. Toward the end of that summer, I lay on a chaise in the backyard of my mother's house in Palo Alto, reading *Going Places,* Lenny's first book of short stories. It was and still is one of his best books: wildly energetic, elegantly written, surprising, violent, and cruel. I remember going inside and saying to my mother, "This Leonard Michaels is a great writer, but I don't think I'd want him as a friend." Over the years I was to recount this anecdote many times, to Lenny's great pleasure and mine.

The Men's Club was a problem of a different order. The book had its own violence and cruelty, yes; but out of the book grew a specter, half-real and half-imaginary, that was more destructive than anything in the book itself. I am referring to the movie deal. This golem-like entity drove Lenny almost literally crazy. He viewed it as his chance at real power and prestige, his crack at the big money, his opportunity to connect with the glamor of Hollywood. It brought out all that was most credulous and hungry and disturbingly naive in Lenny's character, and it did so for years on end. He talked about his producer so much, and with so little to show for it, that we all began to view this figure as a kind of imaginary friend, Lenny's very own extra-terrestrial companion. And then the producer appeared one night at a dinner party.

I had probably had a bit too much to drink. My usual progression at a dinner party is to go from friendly conversation to excessively lively charm and thence to aggressive argumentation, though the progression can be stopped if the dinner party ends early enough, or if someone succeeds in squelching me before I get too far. No one squelched me that night, and by dessert I was well launched into a vigorous attack on the movie *Altered States*, which had come out the previous year. I believe I called it the worst movie ever made, but I cannot now remember my exact words. All I can recall is the expression on the face of Lenny's producer. "I made that movie," he announced quietly. A silence fell on the dinner table.

Now, I could point out that it was rude of the producer to announce this. He could just have kept his mouth shut and we would all have been none the wiser. Still, I'll admit I was in the wrong. But it was too late to apologize—that would only have made things worse. Besides, my friends are used to this sort of behavior. It is part of my known character as a difficult person, this unrestrained tactlessness, and people usually let me get away with it.

Lenny did not. I had insulted his producer (that's how it became known in Berkeley: the dinner at which I insulted Lenny's producer), and he had to renounce me in order to preserve the movie deal. I doubt that this was an actual clause written into the contract. But it was certainly part of Lenny's complex system of superstition—a system which, unfortunately, neatly meshed with Hollywood's own version of magical thinking. If he did not renounce me, he was just *asking* for the movie deal to fall through.

For years Lenny would cut me when we met at cocktail parties, refuse to acknowledge me when we passed on the street, and make it clear to mutual friends that he did not want to be invited over with me. I saw his point at first: I had committed a crime, however obliviously, and he was right to be angry. But when it went on and on, I began to find the reaction excessive.

And then one day it ended. The movie had come out and been roundly trashed. Lenny had recovered from his craziness sufficiently to view the entire episode as one of the worst experiences of his creative life. He had turned against the producer, and therefore he no longer needed to be angry at me: the producer had taken my place as the object of venomous hatred. (Like a primitive tribe or a born mathematician, Lenny always operated with a very precise calculus of emotional equivalences and exchanges.) So one day, out of the blue, he called me up and we met for coffee. Nothing more was ever said between us about either the movie or the producer.

The next quarrel, which began a few years later, was more complicated and less my fault. It began when one of Lenny's wives chose me as the sympathetic ear for her confidences.

Lenny had four wives in the course of his life—five, if you count the longtime girlfriend who couldn't marry him because she was already married to a Swedish baron (a connection of which Lenny was inordinately proud:

he spoke as often and as admiringly of The Baron as he had, during an earlier phase, of The Producer). Of these five women, four survived him, and all four were present, grief-stricken, at his funeral, as were his three grown children. Endlessly infuriating, he was nonetheless a man who inspired great loyalty among those who had been loved by him.

But loyalty of a different sort was precisely what was at issue in the confidences I received from his wife. I gave no advice; I merely listened. (Another friend, also a teacher of mine, whom I have known for even longer than I knew Lenny, has taught me always to suspect that word "merely." But let it pass, for now.) The wife didn't, in any case, want advice, and I wouldn't have known what to advise: I had no inside knowledge of the straits into which marriage to Lenny could force one. My job was just to provide a sympathetic ear, and I saw no harm in it. I have never felt morally responsible for my role as passively involved bystander in the lives of other adults. It is up to them to make their own choices, whatever I say or do not say. I am not their parent or their psychoanalyst. (This, at least, has been my internal self-justification. Explicitly stated, it begins to sound like too much protest. But what is the alternative? To begin viewing myself as a dangerous influence, a manipulator of human souls?)

At any rate, I kept the confidence. But the wife did

not. After that crisis in their marriage had passed, she confessed to Lenny that she had told me about it. (I am deducing this part, as I am deducing everything about the intimate conversation that took place between them. All I witnessed were the results.) Perhaps she confessed to clear her conscience—she had been raised a practicing Christian—or perhaps she confessed as revenge, after discovering some counterpart indiscretion of Lenny's. Or perhaps her motives were a mixture of innocent and vengeful, as they so often are in our morally loaded actions. As I said, I don't know exactly what happened. All I know is that my name somehow came into it.

Once again, I got the whole cold-shoulder treatment. This time, feeling less at fault, I felt more irked. Why was *I* receiving the brunt of Lenny's anger? Did he really expect I should have run to him with the news that his wife was confiding in me? Did he imagine that I might somehow have influenced her behavior? Or did he simply hold it against me that I knew something about him, something I should not have known? And yet how could I have avoided knowing it? When the wife began her confession, should I have held up my hand like a traffic cop and said nobly, "No, I can't listen to this"? Can a reasonable person, that courtroom fiction, be expected to behave so commendably in the face of everyday gossip?

This is pointless. I am arguing with Lenny over an

issue that, even if he were not dead, he would long ago have forgotten—or, if not forgotten, would have buried beneath that ever-rising carpet under which we habitually sweep all our irresolvable difficulties. And if he had not buried the disagreement in this way, no amount of supposedly rational argument (I say "supposedly" because even while I pose as the disinterested lawyer, I recognize that I had and still have the kind of mixed motives in this situation that Lenny would instantly have sensed, if not consciously perceived), no amount of argument of any kind, rational or irrational, would have budged Lenny from his conviction that I had done him wrong.

He stayed with that wife for another three or four years, and then they were divorced. The minute they were apart, he began speaking to me again. Even at the time, even to me, the calculus was evident. As long as he stayed married to her, the anger that might have been directed at his wife had to be diverted safely onto me. I was, in this sense, expendable. It was only when *she* became the expendable one (by her own choice—the divorce was her idea) that she was able to become the vessel for his previously diverted anger, and I no longer had to carry it. If x minus one, then y plus one: it was as simple and as powerful as that.

3.

"I smacked my little boy. My anger was powerful. Like justice. Then I discovered no feeling in the hand. I said, 'Listen, I want to explain the complexities to you.' I spoke with seriousness and care, particularly of fathers. He asked, when I finished, if I wanted him to forgive me. I said yes. He said no. Like trumps."

—*I Would Have Saved Them If I Could*

Let me say a word about anger, since it is something I know a great deal about. If I were asked to say which of the seven deadly sins most afflicts me, I would certainly choose anger. Most of the others do not, in fact, strike me as sins at all. Gluttony and sloth, for instance, may be bad for the sinner's health or welfare, but they do little harm to other people, and pride is a positively *good* thing in many cases. But anger, whose ravages I experience on a near-daily basis, seems to me an inherently dangerous emotion. It is dangerous to the one who feels it (during a routine fit of wrath, I can practically measure my blood pressure rising, sense the veins throbbing in my temples, hear my heart pounding extra-hard in my chest), and it is also dangerous, or at the very least unpleasant, to those who bear the brunt of it. My tendency to anger quickly, a tendency both physiological and psychological in origin, has made all my relations with other people more difficult than they need have been. It has unfitted me for certain tasks—serving on committees, say, or rectifying billing errors over the telephone—that other people seem to accomplish with little or no trouble. It has also caused deep pain within the bosom of my own family. If I could opt for the removal of the organ of wrath, I would no doubt benefit from the operation.

But I would not choose to have it. For anger, in addition to being my enemy, has been my friend—a Mephistophelian friend, to be sure, but one that is responsible for many of my most intense experiences. I am fueled by anger just as much as I am fueled by pleasure, or desire, or willingness to do good. Anger is not always a vengeful, narcissistic emotion. Sometimes it is even a generous one. But it is a dynamo that is impossible to control. My old friend, the same one who warns me off the word "merely," has also said that indignation is a poor master and a good servant. Well, yes, but is it *really* indignation if you can put a yoke on it? In my case anger is almost always an overpowering emotion, brief but intense, like lightning, and it fuels me only if I give myself over to it. If I allow it to simmer inside, it declines into pallid resentment or wan depression, neither of which is of any use to me.

Lenny's anger was of a different sort. It burned like a stoked fire, keeping its coals red-hot long after mine would have turned to gray dust. It combined the fireworks of live anger with the warmed-over bitter herb of resentment and the dark abysses of depression. Lenny's anger was a many-splendored thing. But different as it was from mine, it was something I understood. I am not saying I considered it rational or commendable— especially when it was directed against me—but I understood how it might have arisen, and what it might feel like, and why it was so powerful. The sources of anger in me sensed their counterpart in Lenny and embraced the alliance, even if it was an alliance that kept him and me, the possessors or possessed of the anger, split apart much of the time.

And I think that on some very deep level Lenny understood this. (All of Lenny's understanding of human nature was on a very deep level: at the surface, he tended to be either nuts or indifferent.) I am not saying he could have voiced it explicitly, any more than I was able to until just this moment, when his death has led me to scrutinize the past in a way I never did before. But Lenny must have guessed that I had an anger like his, a fueling anger that could be turned outward on the world to help me survive. And this meant that I, unlike most other people, could be counted on to survive *his* anger.

Lenny and I were both big admirers of D. W. Winnicott, though I didn't learn this about him until after his death; our joint but separate admiration never found its way into our conversation. One of the things Winnicott says is that babies learn to separate themselves from their mothers by learning that hate, or anger, does not kill. As an infant, you can allow yourself to feel independent of your mother—to be angry with her, to hate her, to wish she would go away—and she will still be there when you need her. (This is if you have a "good enough" mother, the kind Winnicott defined and believed in.) I am not saying that Lenny mistook me for his mother; as far as I know, he never stopped speaking to her, not even for a week. But I do think that in some way Lenny knew his anger would not make me disappear. Whenever he was ready to stop being angry, I was still there. This is not something I consciously knew about myself, or something I would necessarily have predicted in advance. But it did turn out on each occasion to be true. And I think Lenny sensed it. Which may go some way toward answering the question I asked earlier—that is, why did *I* bear the brunt of Lenny's anger? Why me and not someone else?

It also explains why I now feel he has violated our compact. The deal was, you could feel anger without destroying. The victim of your anger, sooner or later, would pop back up, like one of those bottom-weighted clowns I had as a punching bag during childhood. Lenny, though, is not going to pop back up. Could it have been my anger that killed him, or possibly his own? Can anger destroy, after all? It is a chastening thought, and very late in the day for me to be coming to it.

4.

"The private life of a friend is to be dreamed about, never known."

—*Going Places*

When Lenny used me as the scapegoat in his marital disagreement, it was not only my involvement in the immediate situation or his unconscious recognition of my durability or even my generally brash, annoying, anger-provoking behavior that caused him to select me as the appropriate placeholder. I represented other values, both positive and negative, that were useful in the equation. I was almost the same age as the wife. (He tended, for most of the time I knew him, to have wives or girlfriends that were roughly eighteen to twenty years younger than he.) Other than that, I was in many ways her opposite. I was Jewish and she was not. I was short and she was tall. I was direct and earthy, she was elusive and mysterious. In all these respects I much more resembled Lenny's mother (who was, perhaps not insignificantly, eighteen or twenty years *older* than he; she had lost her birth records in the move from Poland to New York, so the exact age difference was uncertain, but it was pretty much the same gap reversed). I do not make this comparison idly. Winnicott aside, I always felt there was something slightly maternal in my relationship to Lenny. My friend of the merely ban and the indignation principle also says: All women are always older than all men—and Lenny would have agreed with him. But that alone would not have made my connection with him maternal. There was also some kind of incest taboo going on between us. Lenny was a very attractive man, but I did not experience his appeal as sexual, and he certainly never had any sexual interest in me.

Perhaps that should have offended me, but I don't think it did—though, now that I am examining my motives and his under the strong light of retrospect, I wonder if this can be entirely true. Did resentment at having been tacitly rejected fuel our quarrels? Or were they instead a sign of repressed attraction, like the spats in screwball comedies? I know that both these interpretations seem to hold water, in the abstract, but I cannot feel the truth in either of them. I believe in the unconscious, but I am convinced it always makes itself felt in some way. I have always rejected the idea of false consciousness, which strikes me as condescending and authoritarian. (That is, who are you to tell me my consciousness is false? Or, for that matter, who am I to tell you that yours is?) So I think I will go on insisting on my own version of events here. We were just friends.

If your only access to Lenny was through the fiction, you might have imagined him as some kind of sexual adventurer who viewed all women as potential conquests, all men as potential rivals. I gather he did have a side like that, but I never saw it, except in certain of his stories—the stories about prostitutes in Cuba or starlets in Los Angeles, for example, which always drove me crazy with their strange combination of naive romanticism and wide-eyed titillation. Sometimes he would give me one of these stories to read, and I would always have to say, "Oy, Lenny, not one of these! You know how I hate the ones with women like this," and he would laugh sheepishly and say, "But *why?* Why do you hate them?" and I would once again try to explain. He could never tell in advance which stories would provoke this reaction in me, or perhaps he just enjoyed provoking the reaction again and again and so he pretended, to me and to himself, that it was unexpected. He always seemed surprised when I didn't like one of his stories—not angry, not hurt, just bemused and slightly acquiescent. We never quarreled about things like that.

But, as I said, the side of Lenny that came out in the

stories and possibly in his sexual relationships with women, a persona or personality that was dominated by sexual jealousy, was almost invisible to me in daily life. Among his close friends were many women, one or two of whom had been girlfriends but most of whom had not. So it was clear that he did not always need to be sexually conquering. He also had a tremendous capacity for admiring other men. Of one friend, a handsome scientist with piercing blue eyes and prematurely white hair, he used to say, "He looks like God." Lenny's admiration for other men extended even, or especially, to the men who had subsequently or previously taken up with one of his girlfriends or wives. A friend of mine calls this the "husband-in-law" relationship, and it was this particular friendship that Lenny truly had a gift for. You could see a bit of this in his oft-expressed pride in the Baron, the Swedish husband of his longtime girlfriend; but you could see it even more clearly in the way he dealt with Bob, the second husband of his third wife. Lenny liked and trusted Bob, relying on him to an unusual degree in questions involving his much-loved daughter, who was Bob's stepdaughter, and in other matters pertaining to domestic arrangements with his former wife. He and Bob were also, for a time, members of the same English department, and Lenny considered him one of his few firm allies in that potentially treacherous realm. Another important ally was the husband of Lenny's first Berkeley girlfriend; in fact, I venture to say that husbands-in-law of one stamp or another made up most of Lenny's closest departmental friends. I don't know how to explain this, and on some level I don't wish to. The obvious theories about "triangulated homosexual desire," so popular in Berkeley's literature departments, seem irrelevant to this particular case. Sex was precisely what seemed *not* to be present here. By some act of willed oblivion or involuntary good will, Lenny managed to ditch any remnant of jealousy or preening that might have interfered with these lasting male friendships. And this was equally true, though in a different way, of his friendships with women. Or so it seemed to me, from the partial vantage point I occupied.

One thing that made me partial, and still does, is my own gift, or need, or whatever you want to call it, for friendships with men. When I was younger I had many women friends, but most of them have dropped away by now, or have become dear old friends that I rarely see. The important friendships of my life at this point are almost all with men. Anyone who knows me could think up lots of possible reasons for this: my parents' early divorce, my having been raised in an all-female family, my rather brusque and aggressive and distinctly unfeminine approach to the world, my excessive tolerance for the foibles of men, my corresponding harshness toward the foibles of women . . . it begins to be difficult to distinguish cause from effect here. I cannot explain the habit myself. All I can say is that I have increasingly found friendships with men to be easier than friendships with other women. So I may have sympathized with and even encouraged Lenny's inclination to ignore the sexually loaded element. In some way it must have been my character, and not just his, that was dictating the comradely form our friendship took.

5.

"My father never owned a car or flew in an air-
plane. He imagined no alternatives to being
himself."

—"My Father"

The one night I did spend with Lenny was spent entirely
in driving, he in the driver's seat and I as the passenger.
Lenny was a good driver, and he liked to drive long dis-
tances. Driving put Lenny in a good mood. I guess it gave
him the sense he was getting somewhere, and it also
made him think he was connecting with America—that
mythical America of the roadside diner and the smalltown gas station which New York Jews always feel so cut
off from.

Our road trip started at the Los Angeles Times Building in Times Mirror Square, where we ran into each
other unexpectedly. I don't even remember what I was
doing in L.A. that weekend, much less what Lenny
was. Each of us had been in the city all weekend long,
pursuing our respective activities, whatever they were,
and then by total chance we converged on the Times

Building—and not just the building, but the same floor, nearly the same office—at the exact same moment. (I suppose it won't make the coincidence seem any more remarkable if I add that I rarely go to L.A., and never to the Times Building. That may well have been my only time there.) I remember the expression of delighted surprise on Lenny's face when he first saw me. My own must have looked the same.

"Hey!" he said when we had finished commenting on the amazing coincidence. "How are you getting home?"

"From LAX to Oakland," I said. "I have a flight in two and a half hours."

"Listen, cash in your ticket and we'll drive home. C'mon, it'll be fun. I have my car right here. We'll be home by three or four in the morning."

To get the full import of this story, you have to understand how rare it is for me to change my plans. I am not a great improviser. That seriously understates the case: I am probably the worst improviser of my acquaintance or anyone else's. (I even hate the improvisation part of modern dance classes, which made my life hell in the late Sixties and early Seventies, when the normal embarrassment of adolescence, compounded by the culturally imposed embarrassment of "self-expression," yielded a near-complete paralysis on my part.) I like to have a plan, and then I like to have a backup plan; I rarely meet a disaster for which I do not already have a Plan B in place. The idea of doing something on the spur of the moment is very un-me. But it is, or was, very Lenny. And in this case Lenny's enthusiasm for the last-minute scheme, his willingness to grab coincidence by the neck and wring it for all it was worth, won me over.

The process involved calling not just the airline but also the man I lived with (the man who has now been my husband for eighteen or twenty years, but who was then just my boyfriend) to say that I had run into Lenny by chance and was driving up the coast with him and would be back later than expected. My boyfriend thought there was something fishy about the whole thing, but he didn't know who or what to suspect. So he just let it go. From Lenny's point of view, nothing could have been more innocent. We were just traveling buddies, like Bing Crosby and Bob Hope on the Road to Somewhere, only not quite as comic and with less singing; I do remember there was definitely *some* singing, though.

I don't know what we talked about for nine hours. (It was at least nine hours, because we took 101 and maybe even Highway 1 for part of the time. Even if the ramrod-straight Highway 5 had been finished by then, and I don't think it was, Lenny would never have opted for such a streamlined, unpicturesque route.) Sometimes we listened to the radio, but no station lasted long. Once or twice we stopped for a bite to eat. But mostly we just drove into the darkness and chatted. I remember feeling then for the first time what I often thought since: that though Lenny couldn't be bothered to retain any of the details most other people would have used to describe or characterize me—though he probably couldn't even have told you what color my hair was or how many siblings I had or where I went to college—he understood who I was at a very profound level. He knew a version of me that I knew; or (and perhaps this comes to the same thing) he made me feel that I was known.

The other thing I realized during that road trip was that the nature of my closeness to Lenny depended on not getting too close. I don't mean that he kept people out. On the contrary. His tendency, especially with wives and girlfriends, but also sometimes with other friends, including male friends, was to swallow them up whole, so that he confused them with himself. And once they became him, or part of him, they were eligible for all the criticism, hatred, and coruscating anger he routinely directed at himself. So the only way to stay good friends with Lenny was to stay at the right distance: not so far away that you failed to get the full warmth of the personality, but just outside swallowing range.

6.

"It was a nice day. I felt only a little miserable."

—*Sylvia*

I told all of this to Katharine, more or less, when I first suggested that she and Lenny get together. Maybe I didn't push the part about wives and girlfriends getting swallowed up, but I know, at any rate, that I alluded to Lenny's bad track record with women; there was full disclosure at least to that extent.

Katharine had been my best friend in graduate school, and she was also my business partner for several years. She was, I remember thinking when we started our small consulting firm, one of the few people I had ever met whom I trusted to do things as well as I would have done them. Better, really: I used to say that if she were in business on her own, no project would ever get finished, and if I were on my own, every project would get finished shoddily. She was a perfectionist and I was speedy. It was a good match.

Even in her golden twenties, Katharine was not quite a classic beauty—her mouth was a bit too wide and ironic, and she retained a slightly tomboyish manner from her brother-infested childhood—but she was hugely attractive to men, and this caused a lot of problems for her. She was very smart and could do anything she set her mind to, but the problems with men kept distracting her. She also associated emotional pain with passion (I guess we all did, in those days, but she did more than most), so she would stick with a bad relationship long after someone else would have given up on it. She had three long-term relationships during the period of our youth when we spent the most time together, and all three guys were a bit crazy, though in different ways. In fact, Katharine was drawn to craziness like a moth to flame—a man might look perfectly sane on the surface, but if Katharine fell in love with him, you knew he had to be nuts underneath.

Lenny, as I have already said, was the opposite: crazy on the surface but deep-down sane (though those depths were sometimes so deep as to be inaccessible). I know I said this to Katharine in the fax I wrote to her about Lenny; she saved the fax, and she often reminded me of that line. But I am getting ahead of myself, and I want to tell this story properly.

Katharine had by this time left Berkeley and moved to Italy, where she was running a struggling but ultimately successful business as a general contractor who designed and built old-style Umbrian houses. (Her work was technically called rebuilding, because the Italian law limited construction in that area to sites that had already held houses, but when Katharine showed me photos of some of these "houses" she was scheduled to "rebuild," all I could see were piles of rubble.) She had recently made a final break with the third and possibly craziest of the long-term boyfriends, and she was living out in the Umbrian countryside by herself. One day in the late fall I got a long, rather mournful fax from her, bemoaning the fact that she had all this beauty around her and no one to share it with.

I was thinking about Katharine's fax as I headed off on my daily trip to pick up my business mail, and I was probably still thinking about her when I ran into Lenny in the post office lobby. I was mildly surprised to see Lenny at my local post office—he lived a couple of miles away—but it turned out he had dropped his car off for repairs and was walking home. He was already limping (it later turned out that he had gout, or some other difficult-to-diagnose condition, but I don't think we knew this at the time), so he asked if I could give him a ride the rest of the way home.

As we got into my car, Lenny began complaining for the millionth time about his recent breakup with a girlfriend. He had been complaining nonstop for weeks (there were three or four of us who received frequent telephone calls on the subject) and at that moment I felt I couldn't stand to hear it all again, so I pre-empted the rest of the spiel by bringing up Katharine. "You think *you're* lonely?" I said. "I just got a fax from Katharine, and she's sitting all by herself in the Italian countryside, wasting away from loneliness." I knew that Lenny knew Katharine, since they had met at least eight or ten times over the course of the previous fifteen years at my house, and possibly elsewhere as well. And naturally they knew more about each another than those few meetings would suggest, because Berkeley is a small town in which we all know everything about one other.

When he heard me mention Katharine's plight, Lenny's face took on a new expression—part calculation, part hope, part rueful self-mockery. "If you'll write to her," he said (but every weighty syllable of his New-York-inflected speech took longer than I can possibly convey on the page), "or, preferably, call her on the phone, and tell her I would like to come visit her, I'll be on a plane *tomorrow* if she says yes. But *you* have to make the call, because I can't take any more rejection." I laughed, and he laughed, but we both knew he meant it. So when I dropped him off at his house, I promised to send a fax to

Katharine that very day. And I did, recounting pretty much the scene I've just described, and offering a few useful reminders about the good and bad points of Lenny's character.

Katharine called me up right away and said she hadn't laughed so hard in months. She said she was going to call him. And Lenny *did* get on a plane to Italy—not the very next day, because it was too close to Thanksgiving to arrange a last-minute flight, but within two or three days. Ten days after he left, he called me from Umbria and told me they were getting married.

Certain of our mutual friends marveled at my rashness. How could I have matched up my best friend with Lenny Michaels? Didn't I feel in any way concerned about the disaster that would surely ensue? Did I want to be the cause of yet another hopeless relationship for Katharine? But I just gave them my line about not feeling responsible for the actions of other adults. The choice had been Lenny's and Katharine's, I insisted. There was no guilt or responsibility on my part.

I realize I have been setting this up as a tragedy, but it was not a tragedy. Not until Lenny died, that is, and then it was terrible. That sort of horror, though, is part of life's bargain, and I couldn't have saved Katharine from it—or maybe I mean I wouldn't have, if saving her meant depriving her of the time with Lenny. They had a little more than seven years together, years which would have driven anyone but Katharine bats, but which she savored in her own ironic and self-knowing manner. It could not have been easy, putting up with his maniacal opinions. Even I, after a while, began to wait for the other shoe to drop. "Are things okay with Lenny?" I would ask hesitantly in an email. "Things are very okay with Lenny—more than okay," she would answer. And I knew she wasn't lying. "We really were happy," she told me through her tears as he lay in the hospital; and then she added, with characteristic rueful honesty, "in our own weird way."

7.

> "About forty years ago, in a high-school English
> class, I learned that talking about literature is like
> talking about yourself, except that literary talk
> is logical and polite, a social activity of nice
> people."
>
> —"Literary Talk"

Having Katharine in the picture gave a new overtone to
Lenny's and my quarrels. We now had a hostage. Unfortunately, we both had the *same* hostage, which is not the
best arrangement in an adversarial situation. Equally
unfortunately, we were both notably ruthless people (I
still am, and only death has excused him from this role),
so it didn't much matter to either of us that we had
someone caught in the middle. Or rather, if it mattered,
it did not matter enough to keep us from quarreling.

All the fights that took place after Lenny married
Katharine had something to do with the petty politics of
the American literary scene. I realize this seems dull,
after the excitements of Hollywood trauma and marital
misbehavior, but what can I say? We had settled into the

duller melodramas of middle age. Each of us was firmly married, with no divorce in sight. Each of us had reached the financial plateau on which we were likely to remain. Each of us had a place, if rather an insecure place, in the literary culture of our time. In fact we had joined forces on that front, he lending his name, writing, and taste to the magazine I had founded, I publishing him more often than anyone else did, so that he was helping to create a forum which then gave him speaking-room. It was a nicely symbiotic relationship, and we both benefited—I more than he, I now think, but not so much that anyone felt cheated.

When I say he lent his taste to the magazine, I mean something very specific and practical. Lenny had an excellent eye for good new writers. He could be wrong—spectacularly wrong, as I discovered when I served on a fiction prize committee with him, and he backed the most egregiously boring, awkwardly written historical travel novel I have ever had to force my way through. But far more often he was spectacularly right, in ways that I and many others will never cease to be grateful for. I call it his eye, but it was actually his ear: he could hear quality in even a few sentences of a manuscript, and he knew exactly which writers were worth encouraging and, just as importantly, which were not. His judgment was clouded neither by political fashion nor by personal charm. He found his discoveries everywhere, among old and young, male and female, pretty and ugly, shy and aggressive writers from all parts of America and beyond. He loved to travel to what he considered exotic locales, and so during a certain period of his life he would accept almost any offer to be a guest teacher at far-flung creative writing conferences. From these adventures he brought back to me the best work he could find, which over the years included the writing of a seventy-year-old woman from rural Alabama, a street-smart black guy from Oakland, a depressive white guy from Seattle, an Asian-Hispanic woman from the Bronx, a Southern California boy (scion of a Hollywood family) who was barely out of his teens, a slightly older Chinese girl who wrote prize-winning poetry as a Berkeley undergraduate, and an unprepossessing, quirkily brilliant, working-class woman from a tiny town in Northern California. Other writers I have known tended to specialize in one sort of protégé or another: waifish young men, say, or pretty young women, or slavishly imitative writers whose prose or poetry uncannily resembled their own. Lenny was nothing like this. It was as if he didn't even perceive the surface qualities of the people whose writing he was encouraging. The voice on the page was all he paid attention to.

Sometimes, of course, and particularly with memoirs, the voice on the page and the person who put it there have a great deal in common. Memoir is possibly the easiest form to read and the hardest form to judge, since you have to remain alert at all times to the manipulations of tone and the distractions of content. As a reader (and as a writer too), it is easy to find yourself betrayed by bad faith, sentimentality, lurid confessionalism, slick charm, and the other pitfalls of autobiographical writing. Lenny, perhaps because he was so hard on his own prose, was not often taken in by such things. Nor did he have the usual preconceived notions about what counted as interesting, or tasteful, or important. Several times I almost failed to take his advice because his description of the project was so outrageous: "You *have* to read this great memoir I brought back from Alaska, by a woman whose face was chewed up by sled dogs when she was only ten."

"Lenny!" I would protest, but he was absolutely right about that one, as he was about so many others.

What he cared about most of all was truth. He could hear truth in the rhythm of a sentence, his own or someone else's. I have said that he taught me very little about creative writing, but that was in the classroom. In his writing, by example, he taught me a great deal, and whenever I now find myself trying to set down a particularly truthful sentence, it sounds to my ear more like Lenny's work than like my own.

But I was going to say something about the petty quarrels of our last—*his* last—years. I don't have the heart at this point to go into the precise circumstances of all of them. So I will confine myself to one exemplary case, a single example of our late-stage spats.

As so often with Lenny, the first wave of the ensuing storm was a review in the *New York Times*. Lenny had an odd and not entirely healthy relationship with the *New York Times Book Review*. Thom Gunn once said in a poem about his mother, "She made me and she marred me," and Lenny could have said much the same about the *NYTBR*. His first three books blasted off to success in its pages. I can still remember the handsome photo of him that appeared on the cover in the issue that anointed *I Would Have Saved Them If I Could* one of the most exciting story collections of our time. *Going Places* and *The Men's Club* got equally high praise. But then "they" began to turn against him.

Since I have written for the *Times Book Review* myself on occasion, I know that there isn't really any monolithic they behind the individually expressed opinions. It's true that the editors have ways of conveying to you that one

or more of them really like a book; you can tell during the assigning phone call when enthusiasm is what's
hoped for. But I've never encountered or even heard of a
Times editor soliciting a negative review. And though
they have occasionally killed excessively nasty reviews by
freelancers, there are certain in-house critics whose positions are so powerful that the *Book Review* editors have
no choice but to publish their opinions.

Two of these went after Lenny. The first, Anatole Broyard, eviscerated *Shuffle*—a book I quite like, at least in
places—in a way that struck everyone, even at the time,
as deeply personal. (Another writer of my acquaintance
guessed that Lenny must have slept with one of Broyard's girlfriends to have produced such a reaction; this is
what I mean by petty literary politics.) Lenny went nuts
over the Broyard review, but somehow I don't remember
living through it with the same intensity as the subse-
quent bad review. Perhaps the Broyard atrocity occurred
during one of the periods when Lenny already wasn't
speaking to me, so I only felt the shockwaves at second
hand. Or maybe Broyard's almost immediate death from
prostate cancer appeased Lenny's rage more quickly
than usual. Or possibly I have just forgotten the details of
the earlier offense because they have been replaced in my
mind by the similar details of the later one.

This time the critic was Richard Eder, and though the review was less wildly off-subject, it too had a very nasty personal streak. The book under consideration was *Time Out of Mind,* a selection from Lenny's partly fictionalized journals—not my favorite book of his, but still, miles better than *The Men's Club,* which an earlier incarnation of the *NYTBR* had praised to the skies. So it did seem unfair that this better, later book should have been treated badly. Any writer would have been wounded.

Lenny was not just any writer, though. He began to talk about initiating a libel suit. I tried to explain to him about the First Amendment, and so did Katharine, but I don't think any of it sank in. He went around in a semi-permanent rage, muttering about his enemies. He flailed about for forms of revenge. One of the most effective ploys, he decided, would be to take out an ad for himself in the magazine I edited, a little quarterly seen by about ten thousand people.

I suggested to Lenny that an obviously non-publisher-sponsored ad in *The Threepenny Review* would not reverse the effects of a bad review in the *New York Times.* Our thousands of readers could hardly weigh against their millions, and besides, it would look undignified. Also, I didn't want him to waste his four hundred dollars (he was going to pay me out of his own pocket) on what I knew was a futile gesture. "Just forget about it and finish the next book," I advised him.

Meanwhile, I was talking to the people I knew at the *Book Review,* trying to find out how this bad review had slipped by in the first place and hinting that perhaps they could be more circumspect next time. I doubt my interference had any direct effect, but you never know what will work in such cases, and probably all Lenny's friends were engaged in the same kind of covert lobbying; anyway, for whatever reasons, his next book, a small-press collection of stories called *A Girl with a Monkey,* did get a good review in the *Times.*

By this time, though, Lenny wasn't speaking to me again. It took me a number of months to realize this, because he was living in Italy during most of the year, so I wouldn't have been talking to him anyway, and even a prolonged email silence wasn't unusual. I had no idea he was mad at me until he came back to Berkeley and, after a week, I learned from a mutual friend that he was in town. How weird, I thought, that he hasn't called me. (Katharine, I knew, had stayed behind in Italy to work.) Still suspecting nothing, I called Lenny to set up a lunch.

I could tell right away from his tone that something was wrong, but he wouldn't tell me what it was during that first conversation. All I could gather was that he didn't want to speak to me. I was so shocked I got off the phone right away. Then I emailed Katharine to see if she knew what the problem was.

She didn't, or couldn't, tell me, but the words with which she attempted to dissociate herself from Lenny's anger, something along the lines of "I can't speak about or in any way be responsible for this side of his life," were enough to confirm my suspicion that he was indeed angry at me. I called him up again, and this time I demanded to know what was going on. Pressed, he responded (he was not—he was *never*—the kind of monster who simply slammed down the phone) and told me that I had turned against him in his hour of need. I had refused to run the ad in *The Threepenny Review* when that was the only thing that would have helped him, and I had thereby joined forces with his enemies.

At this, I blew up. "Okay, now *I'm* mad," I yelled into the telephone. I told him about all my calls to the *New York Times* on his behalf. I argued that I had not refused to run the ad but had simply advised against it. I did everything I could to make my case, but I did so in a tone that suggested he was the perpetrator and I was the aggrieved victim. Two could play at this game, I thought, and when the phone conversation was over, that's how we left it. We were *both* not speaking to each other.

About six or nine months later, Katharine came through town on her own. We had one of our usual long, satisfying lunches in which the conversation ranged over everything but the quarrel between me and Lenny. Finally I brought it up—obliquely, hesitantly—and she answered by telling me a dream she had had the night before. "I dreamed you and Lenny were speaking to each other again," she said. "And when I woke up and realized it wasn't true, I burst into tears."

I don't know if she told this dream to Lenny as well. I never understood their marriage sufficiently to know whether words like this could pass between them, or whether she just needed to leave him alone in his wounded state. But a few days later I received an email in which Lenny said (and though I am quoting from memory, I am pretty sure the words are close to exact): "I am sitting here alone in the Umbrian countryside, surrounded by natural beauty, and the effect of this solitude and quiet is to make me feel that I am no longer angry at you for what I thought you did." The message was very carefully worded so as to evade either apology or confession of error—it left open, for instance, the question of whether I actually did what he thought I did—but I was ready by this time for a declaration of peace, and I even admired and was amused by the delicacy of the phrasing. Lenny was completely himself still; that was the bad news but also the good news. I instantly responded that I was delighted to hear from him, and we went on from there.

It is only now, thinking about this quarrel years after it took place, that I begin to see that Lenny's view was not completely crazy. Why *didn't* I agree to run that ad? I say I was trying to protect Lenny's interests, but how does that fit in with my much-vaunted principle of allowing adults to make their own mistakes? Perhaps he was right on some level, and I was afraid to be seen taking his side so openly against the *New York Times*. It sounds too naked and craven when I put it that way, but I suspect that what Lenny saw in me, that grain of betrayal that he magnified into a whole loaf, may in fact have been there. We had, after all, a very complicated relationship by this time, and yet I never even thought to look twice at my motives in regard to him. Quite possibly they were less innocent than I imagined, if less vicious than he imagined.

8.

"He lets himself get away with nothing, not even
his desire to be touched, and where another mind
would stop, blind to its feeling, Brodkey's persists
toward that place, the weird planet on which we
really do live, feeling meaning."

—"To Mean to Feel"

Lenny is not the only difficult friend I ever had. There
were others with whom I had quarrels and reconciliations. I do not know whether I, as a difficult friend
myself, have had more or less than the average number
of such people in my life; it is not the sort of thing one
compares notes on. In fact, the notion of a difficult
friendship never even struck me as a distinct category
until I began to reflect on it after Lenny's death. Only
then did I realize that there were a number of people in
my adult life who fit into it. (I am not counting childhood
because we are *all* difficult friends in childhood, but the
pattern of vicious spats and wounded silences is something most of us seem to grow out of after adolescence.)

The difference was that I sooner or later dispensed

with all my other difficult friends. The cost of keeping them was just too high. I was aware of having to swallow my pain or my anger or my sense of impatience whenever we overcame our differences and got together again. The thing is, we never really overcame our differences: there was always a slight coolness, something kept in reserve, at least on my part and I think on theirs. Whereas with Lenny all was forgiven every time, though "forgiven" seems precisely the wrong word for the kind of instantaneous forgetting he and I were able to practice.

"But you haven't forgotten," I can hear you saying. "If you had truly forgotten, you would not be able to trot out this list of quarrels at such length. On the contrary, every detail of every disagreement seems to have burnt itself into your memory."

Well, yes. I do, on a rational level, recall the fights, in all their gory detail, and at any point in the past twenty years I could probably have summoned up the mental record and read aloud from the transcript. And I believe that Lenny, though he was a much less detail-minded person than I, also remembered everything. If I had, for instance, ever said the words "movie producer" or "New York Times" in his hearing, he would have rolled his eyes in exactly that way I pictured when I thought of his possible response to Louisa's question about burial or cremation. That eye roll of Lenny's, which was less like a human expression than that of a terrified horse, meant *Pain is in the offing—I can feel it coming—Please avert the thought*. It was Lenny's way of saying, "The horror! The horror!" and "Ahfuhgeddaboudit," all at once.

So on a conscious, superficial level, we could both recall the history. But on a deeper level, that level where Lenny operated best (and perhaps, if I am honest with myself, where I did too), the slate had been wiped clean. There was no lingering impediment to the friendship; it was as strong after each quarrel as it had been before.

I think this was because Lenny was an essentially lovable person and my other difficult friends were not. In their case, after the last slammed-down phone or unanswered letter or parting grimace of rage (and in every case there was a last one, for they are all gone from me now), I was not sorry to see them go. I could live without them. Whereas Lenny always left a noticeable gap, an empty place in my life that needed to be filled. Difficult as he was, he was also a terrific friend. After his death, I was talking with another longtime friend of his about the various writers we knew who had died recently, leaving holes in our small literary and personal world. "So-and-so was a real jerk," she said about one of them. "Well," I said hesitantly, "Lenny could be a jerk at times too," and she immediately responded, "Oh, but Lenny was wonderful." She did not say, "No, Lenny was wonderful"—she was not, in that sense, contradicting me. She meant (and I understood her exactly) that even if he behaved badly at times, he was still wonderful. I think many of his friends felt that way.

I have had other friends who died and who, in dying, took away a sizable part of my Berkeley life. Berkeley is like that; it's a small enough town, and a static enough town, that individuals make a big difference to it. When we lose people, we tend to feel the loss permanently, and no newcomer can ever quite fill the space. In the last decade or so, in particular, we—by which I mean we middle-aged longtime settlers—have been losing people with increasing frequency: Bill Nestrick, Henry Mayer, Mike Rogin. . . . Each was struck down far too early (they all died younger than Lenny, in fact), and each left a gaping hole in part of my social world. But I was not as close to any of these people as I was to Lenny, so their deaths, even though they shocked and saddened me, did not leave me feeling as bereft as I do now.

It is a peculiar kind of bereavement, though, more lasting than it is intense. There are other people—and not just my husband and my son—whose deaths would murder life for me. I would not, for instance, particularly care to survive my friend Arthur, with whom I speak on the telephone just about every day, sometimes more than once. And there are other friends whom I miss viscerally whenever they leave town, and whose presence, in some form or other, is crucial to what I think of as my daily life.

Lenny was not like this. I did not especially miss him when he was in Italy. I did not even miss him, in any very tangible way, when we were enduring one of our silent periods. That's the oddest thing about those quarrels: in my memory, there is very little pain associated with them. Embarrassment, yes; annoyance, yes; but not pain. I was accustomed to Lenny's absence and could live with it, because on some level I felt that he was always out there, even if temporarily inaccessible to me. I am not sure how well I can live with the thought that he is never coming back.

9.

> "The sight of him was mysterious news, like
> myself surprised in a mirror, at once strange and
> familiar."
>
> —"Sticks and Stones"

It's true that Lenny was more difficult for me than he was for some of his other friends. I don't mean he was more difficult *to* me, in the sense of being ruder, more angry, more vengeful. Lenny was a bit of an equal-opportunity maniac, in that way. He carried his cloud of obsessiveness around him like Pigpen's cloud of dust in the old *Peanuts* comic strips, and if you happened to come within range, that was just your tough luck. It was nothing personal (except insofar as *everything* with Lenny was personal—but the person, in that case, was him and not you). I know perfectly well that the quarrels I had with him were not the only ones or even the worst ones he had. But they required something of me that was not easy for me, in particular, to supply. I hesitate to call it forgiveness, because I do not really believe in forgiveness (not, at least, the Christian variety we are always being recommended to practice). I wouldn't call it tolerance, either, because both Lenny and I were notoriously intolerant, of each other and everything else; it was one of the qualities we consciously shared. Perhaps the word I am searching for is flexibility.

I have always been remarkably inflexible. Even as a child, I had fixed ideas and fixed preferences. I take a position and I cling to it like death; nothing can budge me, neither argument nor evidence, until enough time passes and I am ready to budge by myself. As a critic, I have found this to be both my strongest asset and my greatest weakness. I know right away what I think about something, and I can hold that opinion in the face of enormous opposition. I can also explain why I hold it, which is where the critical faculty kicks in. But this speed of decision comes with a certain impatience (impatience being an almost inevitable corollary of inflexibility), which prevents me from allowing extremely difficult artworks the necessary time to sink in. If something doesn't work on me right away, chances are it will not work at all. There are exceptions to this—more and more of them, as I grow older—but the number of cases that follow the rule are still in the vast majority.

Recently I learned that I had a tiny birth-defect, a shallow hip socket that had remained silent and invisible for fifty years. (I learned about it when it at long last decided to speak up and make itself felt.) Suddenly I had a key that unlocked years of self-questioning about my physical inflexibility—my inability to do the stretches, lifts, or turns as well as the best students in my ballet and modern classes could do them, my frustrating incapacities and weaknesses in the world of dance. As I lay in the hospital bed recovering from the operation that fixed the hip socket, I began to wonder if there were some similar defect, tiny but ever-present, that accounted for my psychological inflexibility. Would it, too, wear out eventually? Could it be replaced by something else? And did I want it to be?

Lenny was like a stretching exercise for my psychological inflexibility. Repeatedly, over the years, he demanded of me a spontaneity, an ability to retract, an improvisatory suppleness that I did not natively possess. I have just now happened upon this dance-like metaphor, but perhaps it is more than a metaphor, because Lenny and I both cared a great deal about dance. He was one of the rare Berkeley men in my circle—my husband may well be the only other one—who felt that the ability to dance was an important masculine trait. And feminine trait as well: Lenny noticed that I danced well (it was one of the few personal characteristics of mine he ever commented on), and this made me feel that, like my husband, he saw something in me which most of my literary or scholarly or otherwise articulate friends did not. I have said that Lenny did not view me as a sexual being, and I still stand by that, but he did, I now realize, see me as a *physical* being in the world, someone whose quality of movement was central to her identity. And since this is very much how I view myself, it was comforting to get this image reflected back from him.

I am not sure how I felt, or feel, about Lenny himself as a dancer, since by the time I got much of a chance to see him dance, he was so impeded by gout (or whatever it was) that he could barely lift his feet off the ground. But even his shuffling was rhythmic and snazzy, so that he always *seemed* as if he were dancing up a storm, even when he was barely moving. And now that I picture him progressing across the dance floor in this way, I realize how good a title *Shuffle* was for one of his books. It signified not just the random ordering of a pack of cards, and not just the shuffling off of this mortal coil (though Lenny was certainly aware of both those meanings), but also the actual way in which he moved through the world.

Anyway, for whatever reason, whether it had something to do with dance or not, I found that with Lenny—

perhaps with Lenny alone—I was able to exercise my nearly non-existent capacity for flexibility. This may well account for the fact that my husband, over the years, found my reconciliations with Lenny increasingly annoying. That is, he was annoyed by the quarrels (he thought they were all ridiculous), but he was even more annoyed by the speed with which, when the quarrel was over, I would forget all about it. I now think—and I am realizing this for the first time—that my husband resented the way this rare flexibility was being directed at Lenny when it could so much more usefully have been directed at him. But that, of course, was the point. It would have been much harder for me to be flexible within the marriage. I too, like Lenny but in reverse, had figured out a calculus that would enable me to use my difficult friend as a substitute-spouse: to deflect onto him the reactions, the extremes of quarreling and reconciliation, that would not fit comfortably into the domestic setting.

And perhaps I imagined (but here I am speaking of subconscious motives only: I do not view this, even retroactively, as a conscious intention) that my dealings with Lenny gave me some kind of moral credit I would not otherwise have had. I have never before asked myself *why* I forgave Lenny, or allowed him to forgive me, so easily and so effortlessly. I have not thought that it required investigation, it felt so natural. But if I examine my own calculus as relentlessly as I have his, I can see that putting up with Lenny gave me a public setting in which to display my ability to deal with a temperamental man. I am not saying my husband is temperamental in the way Lenny was. On the contrary, to the entire out-side world he appears to be the soul of kindness and compromise, the conciliating figure in the relationship, the flexible one. Only I know (and perhaps Katharine: I think she has a suspicion) how tough and stubborn my husband can be. His is the toughness of passive resist-ance, where mine is the toughness of active effort. This equal and opposite tug-of-war works—that is, the mar-riage survives and flourishes—but it can be hard on the participants. One of the ways I had of dealing with that, I now think, was to relent toward Lenny. If my husband was the obviously nice one in the public version of our marriage, I at least could be the nice one in the difficult friendship with Lenny. Not that anyone else was notic-ing. Not that even I was noticing, until now. But I think something like this was operating, all the same.

IO.

> "Walking down Monroe Street, I approached the
> wavering light of Friday night prayer candles in
> our kitchen window. The shadow of my mother,
> against the window shade, moved from refrigera-
> tor to stove. Everything as it should be. Italian
> ladies with shopping bags and baby carriages.
> Italian kids sitting on the stoops of their tene-
> ments. This was real."
>
> —"The Zipper"

I am glad that when Lenny died we were not quarreling.
And I am glad that before he died I had the chance to see
him in Italy, which was in a way his natural environment,
or rather, the environment to which he was best suited,
possibly because it was *not* natural to him. Some Jewish
writer or other—perhaps it was even Lenny, though I am
pretty sure it was not—used to tell a story about the old
Lower East Side neighborhood of his youth, in which
Jewish and Italian families had mingled freely. "For
years," this writer said, "I didn't know there were two
separate groups, the Jews and the Italians. I just thought
there were the Jews and the happy Jews."

Actually, this could not have been Lenny, because for

him things were never that simple. He could see the dark side of the Italians as easily as he could see the dark side of everything else. But it is also true that he was happy in Italy, and in his life there with Katharine, in a way that I had never seen him happy before. Or so it seemed to me when we visited—my husband, our son, and I—a year or two after Lenny and Katharine had married. We spent our first meal with them at an outdoor restaurant they loved, a place where the chef-owner picked the herbs and vegetables for our meal from the garden surrounding our table, and where we were the only patrons for the duration of a very long lunch. Lenny was expansive and funny and as nutty as ever. Even though we tried to steer clear of the touchy subjects, like Israel, the publishing industry, and English department politics, it was impossible to stay off them entirely, and that's when the nuttiness would come out most forcefully. But Katharine, unlike most of the previous wives, was very good at mildly squelching Lenny's more objectionable opinions, and the lunch was a complete pleasure. Afterwards our son, who, at the age of twelve, had just been given his first grownup glass of wine, commented to me and my husband that Lenny would have made a perfect subject for a recent school assignment. Asked to describe a family member, our son had despaired of having anything interesting to say about any *real* family member and had therefore made up a weird, wildly eccentric grandfather to write about. "But Lenny is crazy *and* lovable, so he would have been just right," he said, obviously regretting the lost opportunity. I did not need nor did I wish to point out that Lenny wasn't actually a member of our family: it was enough for my son, as it had always been for me, that he at any rate felt like one.

But not *exactly* like one. What Lenny offered to me, I now begin to see, was a sensation of the familial without the burdens of family. Families carry with them a deeply engraved history of everything that has ever happened within the family setting. This history is how you are known by the other members of your family, and while that knowledge can be reassuring in a way, it can also be imprisoning. No items of misbehavior are ever forgotten or erased—they just hang about in the grotesquely over-stuffed family closet, waiting to fall out if anyone should open the door. In my own family, at least, no move toward or away from another family member can be made without this burdensome past intruding itself. But with Lenny, the past was only the length of time we had known each other, and nothing else was automatically entailed. I could stop speaking to him without guilt; I could re-engage without acrimony. It was a fantasy version of family, in which estrangement was always tempo-rary and complete reconciliation was always possible.

II.

"In Arezzo, where you go to see frescoes by Piero della Francesca, there hangs a large, startling, magnificent crucifixion painted on wood by somebody unknown. The effect is disturbing. You expect to see a great name, and you're confronted by this crucifixion, impertinently and outrageously beautiful, by nobody."

—"Table Talk"

It was during the trip to Italy, the one to visit Katharine and Lenny, that I first became smitten with Annunciations. We did not see all that many of them (that is, the dozen or two we did see were a small fraction of the paintings, frescoes, and altarpieces on this subject located within a hundred-mile radius of Lenny and Katharine's house), but we saw enough to make me feel there was something about the form itself that appealed to me. Was it the relationship between the two primary figures, the way they were almost always facing each other but somehow facing us as well, so that even a profile seemed communicative? Was it the fact that one was male and the other female, though neither was a sexual creature in any way? Was it the wings?

In the Annunciation I remember best—Fra Angelico's fresco at San Marco, which you come to just as you reach the top of a flight of stairs—the wings are extraordinary. They are so large and detailed that they seem almost like a third figure standing beside Mary and Gabriel. In fact, they take up more space, and matter more to the composition of this picture, than the *real* third figure (it must be Joseph: a quiet, bearded man standing almost offstage, his hands folded in prayer) whom Fra Angelico has chosen to include in what is normally portrayed as a two-character drama. So the fresco is rather crowded on its left side, with a tall Angel Gabriel, his huge, beautiful wings, and a smaller, slightly obscured Joseph all facing Mary across the gap that takes up most of the painted surface. This gap is an architectural space resembling the actual monastery wall on which the fresco is painted—an arched, high-ceilinged, colonnaded room—but it is also a pool of light spreading across the wall and down the floor and filling in the area between the angel and the woman. It is as if the usual white dove or ray of light that represents the Holy Spirit in these scenes has been diffused and magnified to create an intense zone of pure whiteness, of nothingness that is also everythingness. To my eye, the beauty of this picture has been enhanced rather than damaged by the series of small cracks that now run through the space between Mary and Gabriel— as if to stress that this is indeed a destructible wall behind them, and not just a timeless emanation of light, though it is that too.

It is strange that I can feel so intensely about Annunciations without having any feeling for God at all. Or perhaps it would be more correct to say that if I have any feeling about God, it is utterly negative. I don't believe he exists but I dislike him anyway. Nothing in my life justifies this attitude: unlike Job, I don't have a particularly valid gripe against God. But I have managed, in my typical fashion, to convert a rational sense of disbelief into a more personal emotion. Raised as an agnostic, I have instead turned out to be a full-blown atheist, with an intense reaction against almost any form of religious observance. My rational agnostic side is what makes a philosopher like David Hume so attractive to me, but my faith-based atheism makes me much more like Lenny, who was eminently capable of holding two logically conflicting positions at once. Like Lenny, I am personally offended at God's demonstrably bad administrative performance; and like Lenny, I have chosen to replace God with art.

Lenny always felt strongly about the visual arts. I believe he even wanted to be a painter himself, in his youth. Part of the reason he was so attached to Italy was its abundance of wonderful art: it moved him to be surrounded by so much manmade beauty. I remember that when he first visited Venice at the age of sixty-three, he could barely enjoy the initial pleasure because he was already thinking about how much he would be longing to come back after he left. He loved art partly because it seemed to last forever and partly because it didn't.

I don't know the names of all the artists Lenny cared deeply about—he was always surprising me with new ones, and it wasn't until after he died that I learned, for instance, that Arshile Gorky was a favorite. But among the ones I knew about, I thought I could detect something in common. What seemed to attract Lenny, whether in the self-portraits of Max Beckmann or the sculptures of Michelangelo, was art that acknowledged its own tortured origins. He liked—but that is probably not the right word—he *needed* to see the artist's agony written across the face of the finished work; that is what drew Lenny in and made him feel connected. In this respect, all art was expressionism to him, even Renaissance angels and medieval saints. He understood art, as he understood everything else, through his own intensity of response.

About two years before Lenny died (though obviously at that point I did not think of time in that way), my husband and I acquired a painting. We had bought small works on paper and decorative ceramics before, alone and together, but we had never yet bought something as large as a museum-sized painting. This one, called *Shangri-la,* was an eight-foot-long portrayal of a Victorian dollhouse (the walls of the dollhouse were coterminous with the edges of the painting, so all you could see were the rooms themselves) inhabited by elegantly dressed skeletons. In one room, a young girl skeleton in a red dress played the piano while her skullheaded grandfather and grandmother sat by listening. In the bedroom directly above that, a peignoir-clad mother skeleton sat preening at her dressing table while her husband rested comfortably in his rocking chair, his hollow-eyed skull grinning above his smoking jacket. In what was clearly the nursery, baby skeletons frolicked with dolls and toys while a nanny skeleton in formal maid's garb watched tenderly over them. The bathroom was occupied by what I took to be a skeletal aunt, a large, jolly, tweed-skirted character gesturing broadly at herself in the mirror. The biggest room of all, clearly a dining room, held two cigar-smoking men-skulls desultorily conversing over their port; at the opposite end of the room, past the whole length of the recently deserted, white-cloth-covered table, sat a bony-armed young spinster in a ravishing pink gown and a goldenhaired little girl skeleton (not unlike the central figure in Velázquez's *Las Meninas*) propped up in an upholstered armchair. In its shape and arrangement and decor, down to the very color of its strange blue wall, this long room uncannily resembled the dining room of our own Victorian house.

It was clear, from the moment we saw this painting, that my husband and I would probably have to buy it. (We saw it in a show of contemporary Andalusian art, which featured four painters we had never heard of; the painting we loved was by a man named Curro González.) It was equally clear that there were many obstacles in our path. There was, first of all, the cost—about nine times more than we had ever paid for any piece of art before. Then there was the question of where to hang it: in our dining room, obviously, but could our guests tolerate eating under the gaze of these supervising skeletons? And what about us? There was no question in our minds that it was a good painting. The question was whether we could live with it.

And I, on the top of all these other anxieties, found myself becoming uncharacteristically superstitious. I thought it might be bad luck, of some as-yet-unimaginable kind, to introduce these specters into our house; I feared we were asking for trouble. It seems silly now, but such worries weighed on me.

After a few days of fruitless dithering and then delicate negotiating (because some dear friends who had seen the painting when we did also wanted to buy it—that's how evidently good it was), we wrote out the check and became the rightful owners. The huge canvas, when it was finally delivered to us, went straight up onto the dining room wall, the first wall you see as you enter our house. We were excited but also nervous, because although the deliverymen had been vocal in their admiration, our son (who had not been present on the buying trip) had his doubts. Was it still possible that we might come to regret our purchase? We couldn't be sure.

In the days following its arrival, I would come home from the office at odd intervals to visit the painting. It took over the whole front room and gave it a new kind of life (strange to think of skeletons giving life, but these were very lively skeletons). It seemed to me to be an extra window out of our dining room, allowing us to look into a fascinating, dreamy, imagined past—rather than, say, a scary, impending, personal future. My superstitious anxieties disappeared. And yet I still wondered what all our friends would think of it. Until, that is,

Lenny arrived on one of his periodic visits from Italy and, after meeting me for our usual lunch at a neighborhood café, came back to the house to see the painting.

He stood in the doorway and took the whole thing in. He didn't flinch or shy away; there was nothing here that terrified him. Then he stepped closer to the painting and examined every panel, every room. He noted the cunningly carved table legs (of which there seemed to be an inordinate number), and the jolly woman in the bathroom, and the little blonde girl, and the profusion of entrancing household objects, including the barely discernible paintings on *their* walls. And then he sighed a deep sigh of approval. "Yeah," he said with a smile, "it's a good painting."

Since he died, I have searched our Curro González for the agony I find in most art Lenny loved. And, other than the obvious matter of the subject, I cannot see anything bleak or melancholy or tortured in it. Now that I know a bit more about what real death is like, this painting does not seem to me to be about death at all, but about some strange kind of life-in-death, or life-after-death, or life-defying-death. I do not find the painting consoling, but that is not what it means to be. I find it companionable. Maybe that is what Lenny saw in it, too.

12.

"Of course there is all of *King Lear* to consider as a moment of soul. To try to say why that play is good you really wouldn't want the analytical genius of any critic who ever lived, but something more like the boundless enthusiasm of a moron."
—"On *Culture and Anarchy*"

Perhaps one of the reasons it is taking me so long to adjust to Lenny's death is that I couldn't feel sad while he was dying. I don't mean I couldn't feel anxious, or upset, or exhausted, or any of those other hospital-illness emotions; I felt all those. But partly because the whole thing went so quickly, and partly because I was so worried about Katharine, and partly because I kept hoping, long after it was medically rational to do so, that he wasn't going to die, I couldn't summon up a full sense of his impending death until it was actually over.

Sometimes you rehearse experiences beforehand, without even knowing that's what you're doing, and maybe this is what happened to me with Lenny's death.

If I had trouble summoning up the appropriate emotions while he was dying, it might have been because I had misspent those emotions on the rehearsal. I had no idea, at the time, that I was preparing for anything, but in retrospect that's what I seem to have been doing.

A few weeks before Lenny found out he was sick, I sat through Frederick Wiseman's six-hour documentary about the dying. I had been avoiding *Near Death* for many years: it had first aired on television when my son was only a few months old, and since I knew I wouldn't have the energy or the time to get through it at that point, I didn't even try. Over the intervening years I had many other opportunities to see it. I even became acquainted with the filmmaker himself, who offered to send me tapes of any of the movies I had missed, but though I asked for others, I didn't ask for that one. Then, at last, it appeared on the schedule of the film archive near my house, conveniently separated into two three-hour segments, one on Saturday afternoon and the other on Sunday. I knew, then, that the experience could no longer be evaded.

Like all Wiseman documentaries, *Near Death* brings its subjects intimately before the viewer. There is no narrator, except the implicit one displayed in the editing decisions, and there is no story-line, except the one that

naturally arises when human lives are intelligently captured on film. In this case, the normal Wisemanesque
sense of being thrust into other people's lives is exacer-
bated by the setting itself—that is, the intensive care
ward of a major hospital, in which terminally ill patients
are being treated by doctors and visited by relatives. Over
the course of the six hours, you develop strong feelings
about the individual patients and their medical fates;
some of the relatives come to seem heroic, and some of
the doctors less so. The experience of watching the film
is both riveting and devastating, and I wept unashamedly
through most of it. But it was not quite the cathartic cry-
ing that is evoked by, say, a good production of *King Lear*.
It was unmitigatedly painful—so much so that I wondered, at the end of the first three-hour segment, whether
I would be able to bear coming back for the rest. By the
end of the second half, I was so wrecked with sorrow
that I could hardly function in the polite social setting I
had committed myself to for that Sunday evening; in
fact, I excused myself early and went home to bed. I felt
(or rather, I *thought* I felt, because I did not yet have any
real experience to compare it to) as if four or five people
I knew had just died in the hospital.

When Katharine and I were young, we used to amuse
ourselves with Hamlet's line about the actor: "What's

Hecuba to him, or he to Hecuba, that he should weep for her?" We converted it to all our trivial uses—applying it to neurotic fellow-students who reacted excessively to small mishaps, or to overly demanding boyfriends who queried our every move, or to employers who expected us to spend all our waking hours on their consulting project. It was a joke then, though a good and useful one. But as I have grown older, I have come to see it as the central question in my way of thinking about art and life. What makes me care so much about the characters in plays and films and novels? Does it matter to me, *should* it matter to me, that they are fictional rather than real? Do real people become in some way fictional if their deaths are converted into an artwork by William Shakespeare? How about an artwork by Frederick Wiseman? (Or by Lenny? Or by me?) What, if anything, is lost when this happens?

I still like to think about such questions, but I have become impatient with the kind of aesthetic philosophy that tries to answer them. In every case, the particular instance now seems to me too complicated to be covered by a generalization, and this has caused me to become distrustful of theories that once struck me as plausible. I used to believe, for example, in Walter Benjamin's assertion that "what draws the reader to the novel is the hope of warming his shivering life with a death he reads about." Now I am less sure.

What I do know is that I was able to cry for the dying patients in *Near Death* in a way that I was not able to cry for Lenny. Perhaps, as I say, I had used up my tears on the movie, in unconscious anticipation of the event that would require them of me. Perhaps tears themselves had come under suspicion, since they could so easily be drawn out of me by the filmed fates of strangers. Perhaps the demands of Lenny's dying put pressures on me that made tears irrelevant, or unnecessary, or even forbidden. I can't say. All I know is that I couldn't cry for him until after he was dead.

Only three and a half weeks passed between the day Lenny checked into Alta Bates Hospital and the night he died. Before this, there had been almost no warning: a few persistent stomach pains, the decision to go for some tests in Italy, and then, like a hammer blow, the Italian diagnosis. (It turned out to be wrong in the details—they had him with stomach cancer, not lymphoma—but right in its dire prediction.) Against all odds, Katharine got him out of the smalltown Italian hospital and onto a flight to America. The Italian doctors hadn't wanted to release him. "Do you want to take him back to America because you think the medicine is better there?" one of the doctors asked her challengingly.

"I want to take him back to America because his children are there, and our friends are there, and that is where we feel at home," she said in her perfect Italian, and then she looked the doctor in the eye and said, "If it were you, what would you do?"

"I would want to go home," he agreed.

Katharine has always been a very strong person, and a very rational person. She dealt with Lenny's irrationality (and, at times, with mine) by remaining calm and sane. So it was painful and shocking to see how she disintegrated at the prospect of Lenny's death. She did not collapse or yield to circumstances or give up—she organized his care, talked to all his doctors and nurses, got a huge circle of friends involved and kept an even larger circle at bay—but she in some way loosed her hold, temporarily, on her own coherent personality. The Katharine I encountered during those three and a half weeks was one I had never seen before, and I was frightened for her in a way I never could have imagined. People had to force her to eat a meal or catch a few hours of sleep; she had given up remembering, and perhaps wishing, to stay alive herself. She almost never left the hospital, even at night—especially at night, because that was when she feared Lenny would wake up alone and miss her. Every sudden turn in his condition, and there were at least three or four of them, drove her almost mad with grief. I do not say this lightly or metaphorically: what I saw in her during those few weeks was a terrifying abyss of irrationality, which seemed to be her only refuge from the otherwise unendurable pain. She became superstitious—not like Lenny, with his careful calculus of equivalences and exchanges, but like an old Italian woman afraid of the Evil Eye. On one horrible day, for instance, when Lenny was in surgery for seven hours, she seemed to think (but I know she did not really believe this) that if she kept the door to the cancer-ward waiting room closed, no bad news could come through it. I had to persuade her that Lenny's other family members were stifling in the airless room, and that she could achieve the same effect if she kept her back to the door, talking to me for hours on end about the friends she and Lenny had made in Italy, the life they had created there.

During these three and a half weeks, I barely had time to realize anything about my friendship with Lenny, difficult or otherwise. Though I had actually known Lenny for a few months longer than I had known Katharine, I now abandoned him for her—or rather, my anxiety for him focused itself entirely on and through her. This was not intentional, and I think it had nothing to do with how I felt about Lenny as a friend. I don't think it had anything to do with motives at all. I saw that Katharine was in unbearable pain, and so I instinctively tried to do whatever I could to distract or soothe her. It was like throwing up your arm to prevent a blow: no thought was involved, just reaction to circumstances. I could do nothing for Lenny, and so I did not even try to ward off that blow. I lent him a few mysteries to read; I sat by his bedside a few times; it was all useless. His physical distress was in the hands of the doctors, and his mental distress—which was excruciating, since he clearly knew, at least at times, that he was going to die—could not be alleviated even by those closest to him, much less by me. Once, in the first week of his illness, I sat at home and read through an essay he had given me to publish (it had not yet appeared in print) and tried to imagine it as the work of an author who was no longer alive. This was too painful, and I did not try it again. The next time I read that essay, he was dead.

13.

"Writers die twice, first their bodies, then their works, but they produce book after book, like peacocks spreading their tales, a gorgeous flare of color soon shlepped through the dust."

—*Shuffle*

Something odd happened at the funeral. I had only been to one other Jewish funeral in my life, one other burial of a body in the ground, and what I remember from that one is the terrible sound of the clods of dirt hitting the coffin. I remember feeling a *person* was being buried in the ground, and that sensation, that awareness, horrified me in a way I had not expected. So I prepared myself to feel that way at Lenny's funeral. But instead, the opposite happened. As I saw the coffin being lowered into the open grave, I suddenly realized that nothing important was in it. "Lenny is not in that box" is how the thought came to me. It was as if he had removed himself somehow, left by a back door, done a disappearing act. I could not say where he was (nowhere, I would have had to say, if asked), but he was not in that box.

In the first class I ever took with Lenny, which was the occasion of my first meeting him, I did my graduate research methods paper on the poet Randall Jarrell. The class was supposed to involve a lot of bibliographic work, which I managed to evade, but I did read everything I could get my hands on by and about Jarrell, and he became something of a lifelong favorite as a result. He was a good poet, a great essayist, and, at times, a superlative letter-writer. One of the things I remember best from his letters, all these years later, is the comment he made to a friend when he learned that Freud had died. "It was like having a continent disappear," he wrote.

Lenny was not exactly a continent, and his death was not that kind of public event. It was more as if, say, Randall Jarrell had disappeared. Not the man himself, I mean, who was dead long before I discovered the poetry, but the poet and all his work. What if he had never existed? Or rather, what if I *knew* he had existed, but one day I woke up and every sign of his existence had disappeared? That is the kind of disorientation I felt at Lenny's funeral.

But, you will say, Lenny's work hasn't disappeared. The writing is still there and always will be. I tried using this consolation on Katharine during the early days of her grief, but it didn't work then, and it's not working on me now. Yes, the writing persists. And yes, everything Lenny wrote had the sound of his voice in it—particularly the essays, which I think are even better than the stories. But there is something antiseptic, something almost too pure, about writing that survives its author. Everything that exists now exists only on the page; there is nothing left over to infiltrate or sully or drag down the abstract words. They are perfect, in a way he never was, and that is what is now unsatisfying about them.

Lenny was always a reader as well as a writer—I was going to say "a voracious reader," but that is exactly what he was not. He liked the kind of writing you could savor in small bites, without gobbling: poetry, of course, and short stories, but also philosophy (one of the last conversations we ever had was about Spinoza) and unclassifiable works of various kinds, from Kafka's short parables to novella-length essays. He liked things that came in sentence-length thoughts; he particularly loved Montaigne. What he did not like, as he said repeatedly, were novels. Their scale was too crude and bulky for him. He was a slow reader, and most novels did not reward slowness: they pushed you forward with their plots, when he preferred to linger.

I, on the other hand, love novels, as Lenny knew. It was one of our friendly points of disagreement, and we each prided ourselves on the plausibility of our own oft-stated position. The other day I heard some acquaintances of mine talking about how they hated novels; I came up to them as they were talking, and when they saw it was me, they said in a slightly abashed way, "Oh, we shouldn't be saying this in front of *you*."

"That's okay," I said, "some of my best friends hate novels." They laughed, but as they laughed I realized that this sentence is no longer true. I had one friend who hated novels, and he doesn't exist anymore.

If you have a difficult friend, you will discover that a new and paradoxical kind of difficulty arises at his death. It is the habit of grief to whitewash the past. At first, all you can remember—all anyone wants you to remember—are the good things about the friendship. The loss of those good things is the immediate source of your sorrow, so that is what you focus on. And if your friend was a writer, you will have further evidence of how wonderful he was in the great sentences he left behind. But what the grief and the sentences obscure are the very difficulties that made the friendship what it was. It would not be exactly accurate to say that I miss the difficulties. But without the difficulties, there is no Lenny. Maybe that is why I am trying so hard to hold onto them.

Wendy Lesser is the founding editor of *The Threepenny Review* and the author of six previous books of nonfiction as well as one novel. Her reviews and essays have appeared in numerous periodicals in this country and abroad. At present, she divides her year between Berkeley and New York.

A NOTE ON THE TYPE

This book was set in Monotype Dante, a typeface designed by Giovanni Mardersteig (1892–1977). Conceived as a private type for the Officina Bodoni in Verona, Italy, Dante was originally cut only for hand composition by Charles Malin, the famous Parisian punch cutter, between 1946 and 1952. Its first use was in an edition of Boccaccio's *Trattatello in laude di dante* that appeared in 1954. The Monotype Corporation's version of Dante followed in 1957. Although modeled on the Aldine type used for Pietro Cardinal Bembo's treatise *De Aetna* in 1495, Dante is a thoroughly modern interpretation of the venerable face.

Composed by Creative Graphics,
Allentown, Pennsylvania

Printed and bound by R.R. Donnelley & Sons,
Harrisonburg, Virginia

Designed by M. Kristen Bearse